YOU'RE IN CHARGE...
what now?

Seven Essential
Steps for Work
Leader Success

By

Gerald M. Czarnecki

Griffin Publishing Group

Irvine, California

Director of Operations: Robin L. Howland

Project Manager: Bryan Howland

Editor: PeopleSpeak

Cover Design: m2design group

Book Design: m2design group

Griffin Publishing Group
18022 Cowan, Suite 202
Irvine, CA 92614

www.griffinpublishing.com

ISBN 1-58000-109-2

10 9 8 7 6 5 4 3 2 1

Manufactured in the United States of America

DEDICATION

To my wife and life partner, Lois,
who has been my shelter from the storms of failure and
my source of equilibrium in the sunshine of success.

TABLE OF CONTENTS

ACKNOWLEDGMENTS

This book is the result of a lifetime of learning and leading. Sometimes I got it right; other times I had a "negative learning experience." In spite of either, I always tried to grow. After two stints in the military and then a journey through academe, I found myself in an organization that offered me an opportunity to learn what leading was all about. That journey began with an inexplicable piece of luck: I found, or was found by, the most influential person in my professional development. It was a mentor who inspired me with warmth, discipline, and an unwavering commitment to excellence. His name was Gail Melick and although we worked together at the very beginning of my business career, the impact of his mentoring continued throughout my career. I learned much after him, but the core principles were established during his period of influence.

The writing of this book began at the beginning of my managerial career when I first began teaching first-line supervisors about managing. Those days in the classroom helped to shape my views of what leadership was all about, and I learned from every student and subordinate I taught or worked with. As I moved through the managerial ranks, every one of the hundreds of work leaders I knew influenced my thinking and my leadership skills. I owe them all for helping me through my successes and my failures to lead them well.

This book has had the benefit of scores of people who have reviewed a broad range of drafts of the manuscript. Although only I can be responsible for the good or the bad of the book, the improvements from the first drafts are almost entirely a function of the candid, even sometimes painful, feedback from key people. My heartfelt thanks to Dave Heenan, Jerry Porras, George Rieder, Karen Street, Jean Folwell, Ken Gould, Dick Buxton, Doreen Tyburski, Ann Vessels, Julie Swano, Elizabeth Bassett, Kim Stoneberger, Robyn Lighthammer, and countless supervisors who have listened and tried to grow from the many seminars on this subject that I have given over the last twenty years.

I owe a significant thank-you to every manager and supervisor in the subsidiary companies of the Deltennium Corporation who suffered through reading early drafts and who ultimately helped me make the book more meaningful to the people I was trying to help: Work Leaders.

Lastly, but certainly not least, are two who helped clean up the original manuscript. I owe a huge debt to my editor, Sharon Goldinger, who saved me from myself. Her discipline and attention to detail had a huge impact on whatever quality the book has. She took a raw manuscript and helped me make it something that communicated efficiently what I wanted to say. Whatever is good about this book exists because she found a way to make a rank amateur look better. She helped me to learn and, if I ever write another book, she will help me to start with a better work product. The second contributor is my wife, Lois. She suffered through the first several drafts of almost every chapter as it was created. Her honest feedback many times forced me to go back and rethink the book, while her attention to detail helped minimize the serious grammar and punctuation errors that could have survived without her patience.

Gerald M. Czarnecki

Bethesda, MD

January 1, 2003

INTRODUCTION

It Is As Simple As the Word

LEADERS

This book is for those who, day in and day out, lead the people whose work produces results. These Work Leaders probably represent more than 95 percent of all leaders in the workplace. They are the leaders directly responsible for leading the people who are doing the work, hence the term *Work Leader*.

There are Work Leader's throughout the workplace. Examples of this crucial role might be someone who

- Is a lead detective on a team investigating a homicide

- Leads a team of colleagues on a strategy consulting engagement for a Fortune 500 company.

- Runs a section of clerks who are responsible for processing accounts receivable payments

- Leads a team of doctors treating patients in an emergency room

- Manages a production line in the local automobile plant assembling one hundred units a day

- Owns and manages a lawn-care service that has a crew of seven

- Manages an information technology project with ten analysts

- Manages a retail store with nine sales clerks who need to sell a total of $250,000 each month if the store is to make money

- Heads a product management team for a Fortune 100 company with a staff of five assistants

- Leads a sales team of three people that needs ten closes a week to make the month's sales goals

- Leads a team of engineers in a Fortune 50 company working on the development of a component for a new-generation aircraft

- Runs a not-for-profit organization that has a budget of $1,000,000 and employs five people delivering services to the local community

- Owns, manages, and styles hair in a salon with $200,000 a year in revenue

- Supervises a team of accountants who audit a number of public companies

Each of these roles defines an activity that is often referred to as managing or supervising. All managers must be focused on results, and results are accomplished by the people in the organization who do the work. For this reason, the primary skill required to achieve Peak Performance results is to energize the individuals and the team to achieve the goals of the unit. That means you must lead your associates doing the work.

For emphasis on this point we can find no less a source than the insightful author, statesman and intellectual John Gardner:

> Many writers on leadership take considerable pains to distinguish between leaders and managers. In the process leaders generally end up looking like a cross between Napoleon and the Pied Piper, and managers like unimaginative clods. This troubles me. I once heard it said of a man, "He's an utterly first-class manager but there isn't a trace of the leader in him." I am still looking for that man, and I am beginning

to believe that he does not exist. Every time I encounter utterly first-class managers they turn out to have quite a lot of the leader in them.[1]

We believe that Gardner actually understates the point. It is impossible for a successful manager, in the long run, to be a bad leader. People will not continue to achieve for a failed leader. For this reason, the practice of leadership is as important at the first level of management as it is at the highest—indeed, maybe even more so.

A work leader gets the work done, day in and day out and this book is a primer on what great Work Leaders do, not who they are. Much of the literature about managing focuses on the observations that great leaders are charismatic, trustworthy, honest, that they set a great example, and so on. However these abstract terms have a weak link to the reality of the world of work. Here our focus is entirely on helping leaders do what will make them and their organization successful.

Work leaders are the first level of management, however, most also do the task work. People in management often call that type of Work Leader a "working supervisor." Work leaders manage process, but they are probably also part of the process. They are the first line of leadership but also the last line of task orientation as well. These are the sergeants of the nonmilitary world, and they perform the bulk of the direct, work related "people leadership" that happens in the world of work. As John Kotter points out, "What a manager/leader does on a minute-to-minute, hour-to-hour basis rarely jibes with any stereotype with a manager, a heroic leader, or an executive, a fact that can create considerable confusion for those new to managerial jobs."[2]

Becoming a Work Leader

If you were recently thrust into a leadership position, you probably feel unprepared for what is about to become the daily task of leading. Up to now, you were responsible for peak performance in your job. You may have been helping your fellow associates with their work, but your primary assigned tasks were individual ones. Your success was *your* success, your failure also *yours*. Most people who have taken on the leader role would admit that those were much simpler times. Yet almost everybody offered a promotion to leader will grab it.

Most leaders start as people who do the work. They are assigned a set of duties that require them to create output in some work process. They might be accountants, teachers, salespeople, lawyers, engineers, research scientists or even the legendary "mail room clerk." At some point, they get so good at the work that somebody decides to put them in charge of other people doing the same tasks. Suddenly they are a supervisors, or in our terms, Work Leaders. Sometimes overnight, they are assigned a leadership function and expected to do a new kind of job—to lead others instead of doing what they know how to do, which is to perform tasks.

To some extent they take these jobs because they like the idea of being in charge. They may have been convinced that the former leader did not measure up and that they could do a better job. In other cases, they take these jobs because they are convinced that the leader or manager tracks are the only way to achieve the fuller success they are seeking.

Whatever the case, if you are now a Work Leader, you were assigned to the job because somebody decided that you could do it. Once you are on that track, you are going to be held accountable for Peak Performance results and that will drive you to find ways to deploy the skills required. Most management training programs will focus on the mechanics of managing projects or processes. The mechanics of management are important, but all too many failed managers have had those skills fine-tuned by traditional learning while learning little about how to lead people. Joe Batten said it well:

> Managers abound but leaders are still at a premium. Managers manage inventories, supplies, and data. They are numbers crunchers. Leaders catalyze, stretch, and enhance people. They provide transcendent goals, creating a motivational climate.

> Managers push and direct. Leaders pull and expect. Leaders are exhilarated by identifying and enhancing their peoples' strengths.

Despite the many books on management published in recent years, the MBA factories continue to turn out graduates woefully deficient in leadership insights, skills, and hands-on tools. Taking refuge behind reams of data is still appallingly common, but it is no substitute for true leadership.[3]

The decision maker made some judgments about your knowledge, skills, and attitudes. Probably, that person concluded that you could and would succeed, but make no mistake about it, you may also have been put into the job because you were the only choice readily available. That may offend your ego, but it is often true.

Once you are a unit leader, your success is now *their* success. And their failure will be your failure. You have a new identity—a Work Leader. Executing that new role is the story of this book.

Defining Leadership

Defining what Leadership is has been explored by many authors, but we like the simple, yet elegant definition offered by John Gardner. "Leadership is the process of persuasion or example by which an individual (or leadership team) induces a group to pursue objectives held by the leader or shared by the leader and his or her followers."[4] Contrary to the conventional wisdom that leadership is the province of presidents of countries and CEOs (chief executive officers), this definition gives us freedom to use the concept far more broadly. It is this view of leadership that will guide us throughout our pursuit of defining what work leaders do to create Peak Performance for all types of all human organizations.

Leading the Work is Different from Leading the Top

Most of us are fascinated with great leaders and the stories of their triumphs. However, the problem with using corporate, national, or sports leaders as our role models is that the world they operate in has no clear relationship to that of most working managers and leaders. Books that tell us the characteristics of a great leader only help to confuse us when we go back to the grind of our daily jobs. Learning how a mayor makes a strategic decision on when to deploy a police force in a crisis, how a governor decides to reduce the size of a $20 billion budget, or how a CEO acts to increase the profits of a $30 billion company has little meaning to an average leader who is concerned about running a branch office with a budget of less than a million dollars. Knowing that Vince Lombardi shouted at each of his football players when they did something stupid on the playing field or that he created a new defensive alignment that helped set his defenses apart in the National Football League has very little meaning to the director of a not-for-profit who needs to increase fund-raising in order to avoid a deficit for the year. Learning how the president of the United States uses his cabinet to decide how to deal with a crisis in a Third World country offers very little help to a first-level supervisor in the State Department who has a performance problem with her team of analysts.

Many of these well-known leaders of large organizations succeed because they have the unique ability to hire great people and then get out of their way. This concept is often touted as the key to a leader's success, and indeed for many at the top of very large organizations, that is a critical skill. For real-world work leaders, however, that advice could be a disaster.

An organization's results depend on strategy and execution. Organizations must do the right tasks, but they must do them the right way. Strategy sets the course for doing the right tasks, execution gets them done. Collins and Porras in their outstanding book, *Built to Last*, have made the same point, "People don't work day-to-day in the big picture. They work in the nitty-gritty details of their company and its business. Not that the big picture is irrelevant, but it's the little things that make a big impression, that send powerful signals."[5] The top executives set the course; the work leader executes, or said our way, "The work leader gets the work out."

The roles of CEO and a Work Leader are strikingly different but most books on leadership do not focus on the people who lead those who do the work. Work Leaders must delegate tasks, but they cannot delegate the leadership. The work needs to get done and the hands-on leader must be there every day, helping the staff get the work done. There is no escape for the person charged with leading a work group that has daily deadlines and must meet daily expectations. This is a world of task-focused activity, and it cannot be walked away from. Work Leaders cannot simply hire great people and get out of their way. That might work for the CEO of a large company but not for a work leader seeking to meet a production deadline after the power was interrupted for half a day. Work Leaders need active, hands-on, fully engaged leadership to get the staff to respond and to deliver peak performance. Work leaders are likely to be doing some of the work themselves.

In short, a work leader is a person who needs to get work done through others but is also close to where the work is actually done. This activity is what some would call managing. Managers have two tasks: (1) administration and (2) leadership. Administration could be thought of as all of those tasks that we must do in order to get the time to lead: filling out employment forms for new employees, turning in timecards for payroll, filling out budgets for accounting, ordering supplies, preparing reports to other managers, communicating with customers, checking production reports, paying taxes, and so on. Leadership generally means helping the people who work for us to achieve the objectives of our organization. It is about getting the work done through people. Whether you consider yourself a manager or a leader, the goal of this book is to help you get work done.

To be a good leader each work leader needs guidance as to what must be done, each minute of each day. This book is designed to give you that guidance and help you be a better leader. What every leader yearns for are a few simple thoughts about how to get an organization to succeed. The seven essential steps for Work Leader success in this book apply equally to the mother of a family of five, the coach of a soccer team, the supervisor of a team of accountants, the manager of a paralegal office staff, the owner of a five-store retail chain, the general manager of a manufacturing plant, or the vice president of sales of a $5-million company. All of these people have one job in common: they are charged with the objective of "getting the work out." They generally have a boss with a demand, or more politely, an expectation, to achieve some goal and a small group of people who need to accomplish that goal as individuals and as an organization.

7

Getting the work out is essential, and a work leader can make a huge difference in the whole organization's success. John Kotter gets it right when he says in his book *The Leadership Factor*:

> Leadership, with an "l," is of incredible importance in today's world. Its cumulative effect often makes the difference between dreadfully stifling and unresponsive bureaucracies and lively, adaptive organizations. At the level of a single individual, it sometimes occurs in such a subtle way that we don't even notice it. That is especially true if the vision is borrowed (developed not by the individual but by someone else) and the number of people who must be led is very small, as is so often the case.
>
> Needless to say, it would help greatly if we could get more people think of leadership in the small "l" sense" and not just in the larger-than-life "L" sense.[6]

Making the Job Simple but Not Easy

Although leaders do many tasks, you can boil down the role of a leader into seven essential steps. Each of the seven steps is simple in concept to explain, but not always easy to accomplish. To make being a Work Leader as simple as possible, our goal is to get rid of everything that does not apply to the first level of management/leadership and focus on the key elements that will make every Work Leader a great leader.

Our journey will take us through the mnemonic **LEADERS**...each letter represents the essence of an essential step for success. We start our leadership steps with L for love, followed by E for expectations, A for assignment, D for development, E for evaluate, R for rewards, and S for self. The words are important keys to remembering the concepts, but we will explore in much greater detail how those concepts make a Work Leader effective and capable of being great. We are not talking about concepts that are a surprise to the experienced, well-educated, well-trained work leader. Our message is clear: Focus on the seven essential steps and the complex and confusing can be ignored.

In the world of work, leading is useless if it does not result in the achievement of the organizational goal. If a work leader does not get the work out, leadership has failed. Leading successful organizations is hard work. It is not based on charisma, although that quality can help. It is not based on intellect, although it always helps to be smart. If you want to be a great leader, you need to work at these seven key activities every day. There are no days off. Leadership is a full time job, and it requires a complete commitment to these actions—not just believing in them, but doing them every day.

The great news is that if you execute these seven essential steps, you will have a very high probability of success. The bad news is if you lose your resolve to follow the LEADERS steps, you will most likely fail. There is little room for error. This set of actions is so refined that if one step is violated, you will substantially increase your chance for failure. Each step relies on the others. These may be simple concepts, but focused hard work is required.

The Law of Administrivia—
The Greatest Barrier to Leadership Success

One of the long-standing principles in economics is called Gresham's law. It states that if two currencies are circulating in an economy—one a high-quality currency that everybody trusts and believes in and the other a poor-quality currency that everybody thinks has substantial risk—then "the bad currency will drive out the good currency." This means that everybody will want to hoard the good currency and give the bad to other people whenever they can.

In leading, the same principle applies. Call it "The Law of Administrivia": *Required or less useful activity drives out desirable and useful activity.* In other words, people will do the tasks that they think are easy, trivial, and required first, in order to get them out of the way. Then, with the time left over, they will do what is desirable or useful but not required. In short, people will do trivial administrative tasks (administrivia) first just to avoid trouble with the boss. Then they concentrate on that which they know to be useful.

Unfortunately this creates a dilemma since the amount of administrivia grows once the boss concludes you are able to handle what you have already been given to accomplish. Eventually you do less and less of what you want or need to do and much more of the administrative work. Worse still, since administrivia is usually easy work, while being a leader is hard work, guess which work you end up spending more time on? The easy jobs. After a while, all that gets done is the required, the trivial, and maybe even the useless.

Of course, not all administrative work is meaningless or trivial. Indeed, much of the success in an organization rests on process and process controls. However, if they are the only activities a work leader has time for, then they will ultimately hamper the leader's effectiveness. Frequently, bosses forget how much time and energy real leadership really takes. If work leaders use planning, organizing, and control as effective tools to handle the work flow, then much more time can be available for leader work. If the administrivia does not free you, but rather consumes your day, then leadership will be driven out. If the administrative work is effective, then you will be free to lead.

Parts of the Law of Administrivia have been recognized for some time. Saul Gellerman wrote in 1968, "The simple fact is that most managerial jobs are already more than full-time jobs. The typical manager has more than enough to worry about. His typical solution is to arrange his problems in order of priority, deal with the ones he has time for, and just ignore the rest. In other words, that which is urgent gets done and that which is merely important frequently doesn't."[7] What we are adding is that frequently the urgent is not essential to the mission but rather just easier to ask for or to accomplish.

Look at the activities you engage in and determine if they are critical to your efforts to succeed. If you are spending time doing tasks other than the seven LEADERS actions, then you are wasting time. If your efforts to lead are frustrated because you are preoccupied with administrative tasks, then you need to find a way to break loose from the constraints of those activities. You will find leader actions need not be so time-consuming that you have no time for anything else. In fact, if you do the leader work well, you will have plenty of time for administrative tasks. The only way you are going to break loose is when you realize that leader work is the only way to achieve your goals and objectives. It is the "good work." That is the goal of this book—for you to become a believer in the seven principles of all great Leaders and act accordingly by fighting the tendency to be ruled by "The Law of Administrivia."

Getting Maximum Benefit—What's Ahead?

This book is designed to be a handbook for success. It is structured so you cannot only read the information, but think about it and apply it to your life and work. Each chapter follows the mnemonic and the key points are often built into the subheadings in the chapter. Throughout every chapter, you will also find Work Leader Tips designed to give you practical advice on what to do to achieve peak performance results. These give you some tasks to accomplish that will get you moving along the path to effective, practical application of the seven steps, but they will not guarantee success. Remember, leading is simple work that is tough to do.

At the end of each chapter, you will find a Case Study that will pose a real-life situation that could happen to almost anybody and actually did. These studies are summaries of real situations with the names and businesses modified. You are encouraged to read the case, preferably with a small group of peers and use it as a vehicle for discussion of the questions posed. Try some role-playing to determine how you might have handled the situation differently. This is a good way to practice executing the seven essential LEADERS steps.

In addition, a reading list is included for you to review and experiment with. No reader will read every book, but these references will give you a good source of more in-depth thinking on the topics in each chapter. Some sources are referred to in the text, others are references for key ideas, and others are simply good supplements to the ideas in each chapter. As you will learn later, the continuous learning process will be important to your development. Keep the book at hand and refer back to it when you think you need better understanding.

11

Work Leaders Make a Difference, Be a Great One

Even great thinkers of strategy understand the role that the work leader plays. In his book, *Pana Management*, Morimasa Agawa says, "There are two types of management today. One is management for the future. Also known as strategic management. The other type of management is management for the present, the hands-on approach that ensures the survival of an enterprise here and now. Management for the present is what all employees are doing every day in every department."[8]

As the Work Leader, you represent "the present." You must lead your associates if you are to assure the survival of the enterprise. *Do* become a Work Leader who practices the seven essential steps of LEADERS, which are discussed in the following chapters. They are hard work for even the best leaders, but when practiced every day, they will become second nature to you. Stay on track with these simple, yet not easy steps, and Peak Performance can be yours.

Love

Friends Like but Leaders Love

Everything a leader does begins with a capacity and commitment to love. This idea may be disorienting, especially if you're thinking of the kind of love the Greeks called *eros*, what we call sexual or erotic love. Obviously, eros is not the type of love all Work Leaders practice. Indeed, inappropriate sexual relationships with a coworker—or worse, a subordinate—hold the potential for tragedy for all concerned.

The Greeks also used the word philia, which defined another type of love—the love that we have for family. When William Penn first settled in the New World, he named his first and most important city Philadelphia, "the city of brotherly love." The Greek word *philia* was at the heart of the name of his new city, where he dreamed that people would treat each other as brothers.

The concept of brotherly love, or love of family, is a warm and sensitive type of love. It avoids the erotic or sexual aspects of eros, but goes well beyond friendship. The Greeks, and much of Western civilization, believed that the bond between family members in general far exceeded that of any other relationship. Most of us would agree that our relationships with our family members are strong and critical elements of our own personal development.

This type of unconditional love has great emotional and spiritual appeal. Unfortunately, leaders cannot be this emotionally tied to those for whom leadership is our duty. In many ways, the unconditional nature of this type of love can be more damaging than helpful to a work leader. Leaders have a responsibility to be judgmental. Also, they must be focused on the achievement of goals and objectives by a group. Whether you are a priest with a congregation, a supervisor with a clerical processing section, an account executive managing a client relationship, a council member representing your constituents in a city government or a team leader developing a dramatic new software program for NASA, you have a duty to your group, and to your superiors, to achieve goals. As good as unconditional love may feel in any of those settings, any team member not pulling in the same direction is a potential risk to the objectives. You must be prepared to focus on achievement, in many cases to the detriment of an obstructing individual. Brotherly love probably will not help you take the actions necessary to persist on the course to goal alignment and achievement. Indeed, it may hinder you if you conclude that your affection is so strong that it supercedes your duty to the mission of your organization.

So, let's go on to the third Greek word for love, *agape*. This word reflects the notion that we, as members of the human species, have a special duty to love other members of the species. This love for humankind is the form of love that drives activists to support elimination of the death penalty, causes philanthropists to give vast sums to charity, inspires caring people to volunteer in Third World countries, and leads people to help those affected by disasters. We all have that altruistic part of us that wants to give to society or at least to others in need.

This is agape, the fine art—and even emotion—of loving people as members of humanity. It means we have a sensitivity to them that exceeds being polite. It means we pay attention to them, beyond just keeping them from being angry with us. It means helping them just because they are people, not because they are nice people, and helping them even when they find accepting help difficult. It means telling them bad news with sensitivity, not being brutally frank and blunt. In short, it means being sensitive to their needs, feelings, and difficulties. This type of caring is discussed in many ways by many authors. John Maxwell says it very explicitly: "Effective Leaders know that you must have to touch people's hearts before you ask them for a hand. That is the Law of Connection. All great communicators recognize this truth and act on it almost instinctively. You can't move people to action unless you first move them with emotion. The heart comes before the head."[9]

Why Not Like Instead of Love?

You may ask, "Why use the word *love*, when the word *like* would be easier?" Why not say that every leader must *like* people?

For our purpose, the word *love* is more accurate and less confusing than the word *like*. Indeed, the proposition that leaders must like those they lead is flawed. When you like a person, what does that mean? Usually it means that someone's personality characteristics, core beliefs, character traits, or even looks have, for some reason, appealed to either your emotions or logical thought. The person may have treated you nicely, smiled at you on a day you were unhappy, complimented you when you needed confidence building, or helped you think through a personal or business problem. You may have an unexplained bond with that person that made you feel an emotional attraction almost immediately. You may have nothing in common or everything in common, but you feel comfortable being around that person.

In the same way, liking your associates can help you to enjoy the people you lead. It makes you feel good to lead people you like. In turn, since the chemistry usually goes both ways, then the people you are leading will probably like you and feel good about you. If all of this good comes out of liking, then what is wrong with the idea that you should like the people you lead?

Here's what's wrong: How many situations have you been in where you could say that you liked everybody in the group you were leading? If you have a group of two people, then you might expect that you will like both of them. Unfortunately, most of us are charged with the responsibility

15

of leading larger groups. If you are a sales manager who takes over a sales force of ten, the odds of not liking at least one person in that group are much greater.

Let's also hypothesize that the one person you do not like, for whatever reason, is also the top salesperson in the group and has the highest customer loyalty. In addition, that person has the best relationship with the manufacturing division and has always had the highest peer group ratings as well. At this point you might say, "If this person is that good, then obviously I would like her." Indeed that might be true. The opposite happens frequently as well. You can have a top performer you truly dislike. If you have been a work leader for any period of time, you have been in that situation and probably have struggled with the consequences.

If liking is a requirement of good leadership, how can you lead this person? By that definition, you cannot. So what do you do? Your dislike usually becomes a barrier to communication. If you do not like a person, it is very difficult to hide your dislike. The other person will sense how you feel and begin to react negatively to you as well. Slowly, you begin to distance yourselves from each other in an effort to avoid the undesirable contact. Worse still, you will invariably become overly critical of the person. Eventually these tensions will result either in termination or transfer of the subordinate. Bias wins every time.

Like and You May Be Sorry

Just as philia or brotherly love can be damaging for leaders, so too can liking. You may decide to be the leader of only those you like so you will not be challenged by any conflict. That often is the next step along the destructive road of leading by liking. Since you want to like everybody who works for you, you begin the process by favoring the ones you like. In many cases you look past the weaknesses of those you like and become highly critical of those you do not like. The process of favorites or "teacher's pets" begins. Even though your intentions may be honest and pure, you begin purging your staff of all those whom you do not like. Before you are finished, you have a team of people you like. It may or may not be a great team, but you like the team

16

members and they like you. Maybe they are all friends as well. Maybe not always, but this friendship will probably influence your decisions, on occasion to the detriment of the organization. Bias wins again.

What is wrong with these scenarios? You could argue that nothing destroys a team more than a person who just does not fit in. Indeed, that can be very true. One rotten apple can spoil the basket. But what if the rotten apple is one of the people you like? Doesn't that make the problem more complex and sometimes painful? This is especially true if the friend has come to believe that the relationship with you is more important than the leadership relationship. Remember as a work leader your primary mission is to drive peak performance, not have a team of people you enjoy being with. That may make going to work fun, but it may also create serious conflict for you when a friend fails to achieve peak performance. Unfortunately, when this condition exists, leaders have a tendency to ignore the problem until the entire basket is rotten. Again, bias wins.

17

A more common problem is a leader's inability to see weakness in a liked person. We all have a tendency to overlook, if not ignore, weaknesses in the people we like. Indeed, we have a tendency to inflate their strengths as well. As a result, we may be so completely blinded that we cannot truly be objective about performance. Remember, as leaders we are almost always accountable, either to ourselves or to a higher authority, for results that match the goals or objectives of the organization or unit. If we are blinded by liking, then we will never be able to evaluate the performance of the group or an individual in it. Often this situation causes shortfalls in performance or failure to achieve the goals. At that point, most of us will attribute the failure to external factors rather than conclude that we have either failed ourselves or that the team or its members have failed. Bias wins again.

Keep the notion of chemistry or people liking each other in mind. If a team is formed from a group of people who do not like each other, it is important that they learn to love each other. This sense of caring, in spite of the lack of liking, is crucial to team success. You do not need liking to create warmth, you need love. For this reason, when Allen Cox talks of warmth in *The Making of an Achiever*, we assume that he means the kind of caring that comes from loving your associates. "Warmth is catching. It is easy to discern those companies where warmth in management has caught on. From first contact with the headquarters receptionist to the head of custodial services in an outlying plant, a visitor who walks the halls of a warm company and chats with its people, senses the team-play and pride that pervade its atmosphere."[10]

WORK LEADERS TIP   Avoid the Liking Trap

- *You probably do not like at least one person who works for you today. Make three lists: (a) all the qualities you do not like about that person; (b) all the good qualities of that same person; (c) that person's primary duties and objectives. Now evaluate that person's performance against their objectives.*

- *Pick the one person you like best in your work unit and make the same three lists and do the same evaluation of performance.*

- *Now compare the two sets of lists and evaluations. Answer this question: which person is the better performer and why?*

- *You probably have several people who work for you that you like. Are any of them friends of yours? How long have they been friends? Do you socialize with them? How did you get to be the boss of the unit? Did you work in that unit along side your friends, or did you come from outside the work unit? How do you feel about being your friends' boss? How do they feel about it? What would you change, if anything, about your unit and the staffing? What will you change in how you are managing the unit and the people you like?*

• *Have you ever fired a friend? Have you ever been fired by a friend? Are you still friends? What did you learn from the experience?*

Back to Love

The contrast between "like" and "love" is striking and critical. You can love (agape) people and not like them. No one is capable of liking everybody in the human species, but we can love (agape) everybody. As a leader, you must be able to care for all the members of your group, whether you like them or not. Only in that way can you give to your associates the commitment of truth, unbiased behavior, and help in achieving their goals.

Effective leaders have a strong ability to communicate their love to the group they are leading. Regardless of the dynamics of the day-to-day behavior of leaders, the group members must perceive they are being loved. Vince Lombardi was, as many great football coaches are, notorious for yelling insults at his players. Yet, in the face of such apparent disrespect, Vince Lombardi was a loved coach, who earned that affection because players knew that he loved them.

Leadership style is not the issue. Style is a description of perceived patterns of behavior, not necessarily a reflection of the internal capacity to love. In some style or personality types, it may take a little longer to determine if the capacity to love is present, but the lack of that capacity is almost always obvious. It seems that you can always detect a mean streak, or a lack of love, much faster than you can identify a real capacity to love.

Don't Fake It

It is almost impossible to hide a lack of love. Somehow those who pretend to have agape seem to give themselves away. "All the world is a stage," Shakespeare said, and many leaders are great actors. Some acting skill is probably helpful because even the most sincerely loving leaders sometimes have a bad day. At these times, acting that provides encouragement and enthusiasm can often be a very valuable

19

tool for the leader. On the other hand, people in leadership positions who pretend to be loving ultimately create trauma for those being led. It is irrelevant how good the acting is; a leader's actions will speak louder than words or body language. Over time it is almost impossible for a "nonloving" person to hide the lack of human caring and agape.

The Pain of Working without a Loving Boss

Most of us have worked for nonlovers. One boss made me feel uncomfortable just to be in his presence. I was his chief financial officer (CFO) and very early on he made it clear that he knew my job better than I did. He never really had to say anything to cause me to have self-doubts. After several months of this unexplained fear, I dreaded going to see him. The situation was getting worse, not better. Each encounter created another bad experience for me and probably for him as well.

I had a difficult time understanding what was happening to me until one day we were discussing another person, who had caused some difficulties in the company, and he said to me, "I do not trust him, but then, I do not trust anybody. And you, Gerry, your problem is you trust people. My advice to you is to recognize that the people who work for you are just human resources of the business, and you need to use them as if they were expendable. The only thing that matters is that we get the job done, and that means you need to check up on everything those people do." (As you might expect, I was working for a different company in less than six months.) This boss never understood that love and trust were the foundation of all human relationships. In fact, he never could check up on everybody all the time, and ultimately his subordinates failed him and the company. He never evolved into a leader, and he sank along with the company as it went into tragic decline. In this case, their failure was his.

Agape is a state of the rational mind as much as it is an emotion. Loving others does not guarantee that they will love you. Indeed, if you trust people and they do not reciprocate, you will have trouble. That is why some, like my infamous boss, would say you should never trust anyone. It is true that some people whom you love as humans will not repay your trust. Some people in this world are lazy, dishonest, uncaring, unloving or just plain incompetent. However, no leader can be effective without a deep love for people as human beings.

We leaders need to have love at the heart of everything we do because we are responsible for the success of our associates. At times, that love will be reflected in a sensitivity to an associate's anxiety; at other times, it will require high standards and expectations to focus an associate on achievement; at other times, it will mean reinforcing a successful action; and at other times, it will mean disciplining a serious misstep. All of these efforts will require more than just a mechanical effort. They require that extra measure of emotional sensitivity that is embodied in the concept of agape. *Only* when you love your associates can you perform these responsibilities with the sensitivity, compassion, and firmness required to assure successful goal achievement.

The concept of "tough love" is very similar. It essentially means that parents need to love their children so much that they are able to be firm in their discipline process—to be tough, but with love. In the same way, as leaders we must care so much (love) that we are able to reinforce the required behavior through the tough discipline essential to the development of our staff. Love does not need to be soft to be real.

Remember, the objective here is the achievement of goals by your associates. Indeed, not just achievement, but Peak Performance. That means you must lead them to success by helping them incorporate behaviors that will get results. You are the most powerful force in the lives of your associates. If you accept that heavy responsibility, then remember that your love of them will be the best guide for your actions. It will help you to make tough choices between concern for your organization's goals and the concern for an associate. There is no greater challenge than to maintain that balance. Warren Bettis said it very well: "Ultimately, a leader's ability to galvanize his coworkers resides both in his understanding of himself and in his understanding of his coworkers needs and wants..."[11]

Keep in mind that few people want to fail. Failure is generally the result of misdirected effort by well-intentioned people. A leader's responsibility is to help all associates direct

21

their efforts toward a successful result, rather than wasting it on failure. The best way to accomplish that is to help associates find the answers within themselves. When you order them to act as you direct, you have shown them success. When you help them to discover their own potential, you have shown them how to succeed. This commitment is possible only if you have the capacity to love them as human beings who have a right to the dignity that comes from personal achievement.

If You Can't Love, Quit Trying to Be a Leader!

Now the real challenge—should you be a work leader? If you look in the mirror and find that you cannot have agape for your associates, then you should stop trying to be a work leader. If you conclude that you would rather do it yourself than have the patience that love requires to help others succeed, then quit your job as a leader. If you enjoy your own successful achievement of a task more than helping another succeed at the same task, then leave your current leadership position and get back to doing the task yourself. If you try to fake love, you will be caught. If you try to lead without love, you will fail.

As a leader you are not alone. If your interest is in being able to do and say whatever you feel, then being a leader is the wrong role for you. You must recognize the impact that you can have on your associates. As Beverly Potter says, "Your own behavior has an impact around you. Things you do and say (or don't do and don't say) can function as antecedents that evoke—or as consequences that maintain—the behavior of someone else. The more you understand the interrelationships between your behaviors and the behaviors of subordinates, the more you can manage others by managing yourself."[12]

If, on the other hand, you're capable of agape, then you may be ready to become a good leader. True work leaders have a greater joy in seeing others succeed than in experiencing their own personal achievement. They enjoy helping others triumph over major obstacles; they love seeing their associates receive awards for success; they get chills when they see a previously unsuccessful associate achieve greatness. Great leaders, like most people, have egos. But their egos are fed by the thrill of having somebody tell them that they have done a great job helping somebody else succeed. If that describes you, you are the right person to lead and the rest of this book is designed to help you channel that love into those actions that will make you a great leader.

CASE STUDY

"Patricia had had a bad night and the morning was starting off even worse. She was not only late for work, but she dreaded her upcoming meeting with her boss at ten. She knew he was going to criticize her for being behind on her project. Her staff had failed her for months now, but she had yet to figure out what to do to get the project back on track.

Frank, her favorite project leader, had gotten far behind and the turnover in his group had been terrible. Frank was trying everything but was having no luck with his staff. June, her least favorite manager, was continuing to annoy her. Every time she tried to get June to take on just a little more responsibility to help Frank get his project goals completed, June would respond with negative, complaining feedback. She would say, "I am already working sixty hours a week, and I simply cannot handle any more. Why don't you figure out why Frank cannot keep up?"

How dare she try to tell me what I should do? Patricia then would say to herself, She has no idea the challenges that Frank has with his project. I am sick of her whining.

23

Patricia was fed up with the entire project and with managing a bunch of incompetent and lazy people. She thought, Maybe I ought to fire the entire lot, except for Frank, and start all over. Maybe with a new group of people, I could find at least a couple with the smarts and the drive to get quality work done. Then she thought, That may be the only way I am going to get my boss off my back also. If I just get rid of these people in my group, maybe my boss will give me a little more time. I'll bet I can buy at least three more weeks if I look like I am being decisive.

Patricia left work that night feeling very good. She went out with a group of friends from work and they all told her that they thought she was in trouble with her boss. To them the solution was easy: just get back on schedule. Patricia did not share with them her own strategy. She was convinced that they all would tell her she was being too tough, but there was no doubt in her mind that she needed to get rid of the people she did not like, and build a loyal staff of people just like Frank.

After carrying out the tough action she planned, Patricia felt great about her position in the company. She knew that it was only a matter of time and her new staff would bail out the project. However, when she told her boss what she had done, he clearly was not happy with her decision, and that afternoon Pat was fired.

Questions

1. What could Patricia have done to save her job?

2. Patricia is capable of liking a subordinate. Is Patricia capable of love?

3. Is Patricia's loyalty to Frank an admirable trait?

4. Was Frank a good performer? Did his performance warrant Patricia's loyalty?

5. What should Frank have done?

6. Why did Patricia ignore her friend's advice?

7. Why did Patricia fail to see she might lose her job because of the actions she took?

8. Would you like Patricia to be a friend of yours? If so, why? If not, why not?

9. What should Patricia do now?

10. Should Patricia be a manager?

Expectations
Setting the Bar Sets the Tone

"How was I supposed to know what you wanted? What do you think I am, a mind reader?" Have you ever asked these questions? Has anybody who works for you asked them? Questions like these raise the issue of expectations. This element of leadership is where the real work begins.

Setting expectations is the first step on a work leader's journey. From this action, all other actions flow as natural next steps. Where love sets the tone for the leadership relationship, expectations set the focus for achieving future successes. Setting expectations means taking several specific actions, all of which are critical to the success of a leader and in turn, the organization. These include establishing a vision, a mission, a set of core values or principles, a strategy, goals, specific objectives, and detailed action plans. Many management books cover these steps. However, since work leaders frequently must follow a business plan written by somebody else, this book concentrates on those actions you can take right now in your leadership role.

Your goal should be to determine those tasks you must execute to achieve peak performance. In short, as Dr. Thomas Gordon says, "An effective leader cannot be only 'human relations specialist' (meeting members' needs) nor only a 'productivity specialist' (meeting organizational needs). He or she must be both."[13]

Most organizations have goals and objectives. Some may be vague; others may be well-thought-out and focused. Whatever the case, work leaders must expect that these goals will set their day-to-day agenda.

Work leaders do not set vision, strategy, or corporate goals, but they do lead their associates to complete objectives in the work unit. That type of leadership requires helping associates focus on accomplishing tasks and achieving results. Getting the work done within established objectives of quality, cost, and time is the true measure of a work leader's success.

In creating a meaningful set of expectations, a work leader must keep in mind that the expectations must match the goals of the enterprise, and these goals must be goals that are within the range of responsibility of the unit. Waste no time dreaming about how the world could be better "if only." Focus on achieving those expectations that will reward the organization with Peak Performance. Set expectations for, or with, your associates that meet the mission of the unit.

In addition, setting expectations requires constant diligence. Goals set today may not be enough. New technology or other changes in this fast-paced world may mean that next month or next quarter the unit will need to face another change in expectations. Hence, working at expectations is not a one-time event.

WORK LEADERS TIP Ask Yourself These Questions. If You Don't Know the Answers, Ask Your Boss.

•*Does your organization have a vision statement? How about a mission statement? Do you think you need one? Have you made up your own? Does it match what is written by the organization or have you gone off on your own journey?*

- *Do you have a clear understanding of the expectations your boss has for your work unit? Make a list of those expectations and explain what may be missing.*

- *When you set expectations for your staff, how did you decide who got what goals? Did they participate in the goal setting? Should they have been involved?*

- *When your boss last told you how you were doing, what did he say? Were his expectations being met? If not, why not? If yes, then how did that happen? Did you do the work yourself? Did your staff do it? What is your secret for success in meeting your boss's expectations?*

- *There are times when we have the ability to do more than is expected of us. Is there anything you think your organization needs that you could be providing? Have you talked to your boss about taking on that responsibility?*

- *Is there any chance that your boss already thinks that you are doing something to achieve that result? Could he have hidden expectations of you that you have not been assigned in your formal goal-setting process with your boss?*

- *What is the relationship of the expectations you have for your staff to those that your boss has for you? If your staff meets your expectations, will you impress your boss? If not, why not? Is there anything that you can do to make your expectations of your staff more closely linked to what your boss expects of your unit?*

When setting expectations, seven key components will help you achieve Peak Performance:

1. Simple

2. Specificity

3. Measurability

4. Buy-in

5. Team commitment to common expectations

6. Self-interest

7. Raising the bar

Simple Is Better

Remember the old saying, "If you have no goal and plan, any road will get you to where you are going?" That is precisely why we must know our expectations and, in turn, why our associates must know our expectations of them. The best way to do this is the simple way. Keeping expectations simple means that neither we, nor any of our associates, need to have an infallible memory for details. A few key goals, objectives, or action plans are all we need to be certain that every associate has a clear understanding of what we expect of the organizational unit, and most importantly, what is expected of them to achieve the unit goals. Remember, expectations are set so that the leader and the associates can achieve the goals of the organization.

Remember, a few key elements done well can make you a successful leader. The same premise drives the seven "LEADERS" principles. This idea has nothing to do with intelligence. It has everything to do with focus. Every great leader's story tells how a simple strategy, simple plans, and simple execution won the day. Doing a few jobs better than anybody else is what makes McDonald's, Starbucks, and Southwest Airlines so successful. True genius makes the most complex simple. Einstein wrote $E = mc^2$ and changed the world. If that genius can boil his great thought down to a few symbols, we as leaders can boil our thoughts down to a few key words, phrases, or sentences.

Which of these expectations is easier to understand, accept, or agree to?

1. We will process all of our applications so that they are perfect in every respect and so that customers will believe that we are a caring, committed, and focused company that has their best interests at heart and so that they will always be able to trust us and get a product that satisfies their most critical expectations.

2. We will provide customer delight through processing applications with less than a .0001 percent error rate.

You will probably agree the second sentence is simpler and far more powerful. It may not have the same "good feeling," but it is very specific and very focused on achieving peak performance.

Be Specific

If you were the CEO of a business or other enterprise, you would need to start with a vision of what you want the enterprise to be. It could be "We want to put a PC in every home," "We want to delight our customers," or "We want to be the largest company in the world." As simple or as grandiose as you choose to make it, this statement would reflect what you want to be when you have achieved "perfection." It may or may not be realistic to expect it to be achievable, but it should reflect your highest ideal.

Obviously, the next step is to define the mission of the organization. Once again, the CEO probably should do this, but even at lower organizational levels, knowing and understanding the organization's mission is a vital part of achieving. An enterprise mission might be "To manufacture parts for the aviation industry" or "To provide accounting services to the small business entrepreneur" or "As a charitable foundation, to fund a select group of organizations providing support for battered or abused women."

At a lower organizational level, a work leader's mission statement could be "To make the final stamping operation for airframe components" or "To manage the bank

31

reconciliation efforts for all clients" or "To evaluate proposals for seed funding for new projects by existing client organizations." Whatever the level, each unit must understand what it is supposed to do. Either you as its work leader must get this information from "above," or you need to set the mission yourself. Then and only then can you proceed effectively to set strategy and goals.

Strategy usually answers the question, "How are we going to get it (the mission) done?" For a parts manufacturer, the answer could be to use modern flow manufacturing techniques that minimize inventory requirements. For an accounting service, it could be a marketing concept of selling only to franchisees of major chains. For a not-for-profit, it could be a decision to solicit funds from people who have just sold an initial public offering and have dramatically appreciated stock that could be given in a way that has tax advantages. Whatever the strategy, or strategies, the statement probably needs to be a way of doing something, not a specific set of tasks to do.

For a work leader, the strategy concept is a little less helpful but may still apply. A manufacturing section leader might focus on reducing rework; an accounting supervisor might try to develop a system to have automated account reconciliation on all accounts over a given size. In the case of a proposal section manager for a consulting firm, the strategy might focus on finding ways to identify key factors impacting the customer/prospect decision. These are all concepts of how to approach the mission, not specific actions.

WORK LEADERS TIP — What Does an Expectation Look Like?

Anything that your staff routinely does to achieve the goals of the enterprise is a potential area for expectation setting. Do not set expectations for tasks that will not contribute directly to the success of your unit.

Below are some examples of tasks you should establish expectations for:

Number of tax returns completed by day

Customers serviced per day

Errors made per hour

Applications processed per day

Parts produced per hour

Lawns cut per day

Incoming phone calls handled per hour

Sales made per month

Cars repaired per day

Lines of code written per hour

Haircuts completed per hour

Accounts reconciled per hour

Parts produced per hour

Complaints handled per hour

Prescriptions filled per day

Orders processed per hour

Applications processed per hour

Complaints resolved per hour

33

The Devil Is in the Details—Measurement Matters

Vision and strategy are generally in the province of top management, but at the level of the work leader, the key words are *goals*, *objectives*, and *action plans*. Detail is king. Virtually everybody is involved in the setting of expectations. At this level, we must establish very specific tasks that we think must be done for the organizational mission to be accomplished. For a CEO, the task could be achieving growth in sales of 25 percent. For a work leader in charge of sales, that goal could be further refined: to call on thirty prospects a month, to sign up at least two new customers per month who order at least $100,000 in new parts to be delivered within three weeks of the order date. For a section supervisor in a manufacturing plant, the goal could be to produce an average of five hundred airfoils per day, with a less than .005 percent rework rate, at a cost of less than $35 per unit, and with 99.9 percent delivered by the committed delivery date. For an office manager, the goal might be to have all current day documents filed by the end of each working day.

Setting these kinds of very specific, detailed, and measurable goals and objectives is the essence of successful leadership. Ambiguous expectations create ambiguous results. If expectations are not measurable, everybody can claim that an objective has been met no matter what the result.

The final component of setting expectations must be that you can find some way to be able to evaluate the performance against the expectations. Chapter 5 will present more about evaluation, but the process begins with setting expectations. Your goal is to be certain that you eliminate ambiguity early, since ambiguity will be painfully obvious in evaluations.

The standard advice on this point is to set goals, objectives, and action plans that can be measured quantitatively. The practical reality is that many expectations, particularly behavior-related expectations, are very difficult to quantify.

Make certain that when you set the expectations you have already decided how you are going to measure the performance. Too many times after a decision to measure an expectation has been implemented, it is discovered that measuring the expectation is too time-consuming, too costly, or too inaccurate. In that case, you will spend more time measuring the results than you will actually getting the results. Always make sure that measurement is easy and obvious. If your staff thinks that the results may be disputed, then you can be certain they will be.

The best advice is to make an effort to find an easy yet meaningful way to quantify the metric. If it comes quickly, then use it. If the goal is more qualitative than quantitative, then forget about measuring it. But remember, without a measure you make your job much harder when you get to the evaluation stage, and you make developing an associate's core abilities more difficult as well.

WORK LEADERS TIP — Set Expectations That Are Specific, Measurable, and Unambiguous!

Using some of the examples from an earlier tip, here are some thoughts about how to make the goals specific, measurable and effective:

Tax returns prepared. *Each accountant will complete an average of ten tax returns per day during the tax season.*

Customers serviced. *During each quarter, each branch customer service representative will process to completion an average of twenty-five walk-in customers per day with an average score of "Highly satisfied" on the customer satisfaction survey.*

Errors made. *Each machine in the production unit will produce at an average reject rate of not greater than .005 percent.*

Sales calls made. *Each salesperson will make a minimum of 250 calls to prospects from the lead list provided by the corporate office.*

Haircuts completed. *Each stylist will, each week, complete an average of 2.7 cuts per hour with a redo rate of not greater than .5 percent.*

Orders processed. *Each processor will process to shipping a minimum of 99 percent of all orders received in a day.*

35

Work leaders must know what is expected and, in turn, must be certain that their associates know what is expected of them. If associates do not know the expectations, then they will set their own. If they set their own, they are not responding to the goals of the organization; they are responding to their own goals. When the time comes to evaluate performance, then no standard will apply. Having associates guess at what is expected is absurd. It is our duty as leaders to assure that their goals coincide with those of the organization.

Buy-In

The issue of "buy-in," or assent, has been a hot topic in business for a long time. Your success will be largely dependent on how well you get that buy in, but it is also important not to waste your time. Any idea that you take to your staff will almost always be met with resistance. You need to be ready for that. Also be prepared for the possibility that, no matter what you say, no matter how persuasive you and others may be, you will not get agreement from every member of the staff to a new idea or a new expectation. You may want agreement, but you should be prepared to settle for less. Think about the process this way:

1. **Understanding** is when associates have no questions about the expectation. They know what it is, what it means, what they are expected to do, and what it will take to achieve results that meet the expectation.

2. **Acceptance** is when staff members have concluded that an expectation can be used to determine success and that you and the organization have the right to establish the expectation. They will not fight the expectation and will work to meet it.

3. **Agreement** is when staff members understand, accept, and also agree with the expectation. In short, they believe it is the correct measure of performance.

No doubt, the ideal level of buy-in is agreement, but if you only get acceptance, take it and move on. What you have gotten is recognition that the expectation works, even though the staff members would not have chosen it. In the long run, if the expectation is fair, staff members will probably begin to agree. Save your powers of persuasion for another day and another issue.

WORK LEADERS TIP — Practice Understanding, Acceptance, and Agreement

You must make certain that your associates know what is expected and what they need to do to achieve success. Buy-in is only possible when clarity exists. Ask yourself these questions to be certain they understand. Remember understanding is an essential first step to acceptance.

- *Pick the one subordinate who has been achieving the least and identify the expectations you have for that person. Does she know precisely what you expect? If not, did you make the goals clear? Are they written down?*

- *Pick the best subordinate you have and write down the expectations she has most effectively achieved. How do you know that the performance is effective? What is the measurement you used? Does that associate really understand? If so, what did you do differently than with the one who does not understand?*

- *You probably have some personal tasks that contribute to the results of the unit. How much of the performance of your work unit is completely tied to your personal performance? Is there an associate who should be doing the job, but is not because that associate does not understand or accept your assignment? Have you explained her need to accept that assignment?*

- *Most Work Leaders have a secret wish such as, "If only Joe could do that." Do you have such a secret wish? What has kept you from expecting Joe to accomplish that goal? What can you do to get that task assigned to Joe? Does Joe understand his assignment?*

- *Do all members of your work unit have a clear set of expectations? Do they understand and accept the expectations or have you failed to effectively communicate them? Make a list of each person who may not know what the expectations are for his or her job and create that list of individual expectations. Once you have completed that list, what do you plan to do with it?*

Great Teams Have Common Expectations of Members

As a leader you must communicate another type of expectation to your associates—what you expect of them as members of the organization. You must make certain that each person in your organization knows what the rules are for being part of the team. These rules could be as simple as "Be at work on time every day" or as complex as "We expect every person to hit a specific quality standard for output, a certain volume standard for productivity, and a certain cleanliness standard at the work station."

It is essential that all team members remember that a team works together and that an individual must bend to the benefit of the team. Norm Augustine talks about working for the good of the team:

> *Teamwork is the fabric of effective business organizations. Soloists are inspiring in opera and perhaps even in small entrepreneurial ventures, but there is no place for them in large corporations. This is most assuredly not to say there is no place for the individualist, only that it is necessary for members of the team to be willing to suppress individual desires for the overall good of the team.*[14]

The team rules could include clear statements of expectations about integrity, courtesy, team participation, safety, and a host of other traits that set the tone for everyday activity. They need to know how you want to deal with conflict, what you expect from the group discussions, or how you expect them to share feedback with each other. In short, they need to know how you expect the team to work as a work unit.

Self Interest—What Is in It for Me?

Keep in mind that your staff members are probably not trying to get you a promotion. If they think you are a great leader, they probably would prefer you to stay right where you are. If they don't, they probably would like to see you fired. Even if they think that you are the best boss they have ever had, your success is not likely to be their highest priority.

Actually, they probably want a promotion themselves. It's not that all of your staff members are self-centered and uncaring. They are looking forward to their own future, even if that means next week. Whatever your expectations of them, they are not likely to try to achieve them because it will make you look good or make the company beat the competition. They are much more likely to try to achieve organizational peak performance expectations or goals if they find a way to achieve their own personal goals as well. They are probably much more interested in what they will get from that success. That is fine as long as the organization wins as well; hence when you set expectations, make certain that staff members know what it means to them if they achieve the standard.

Imagine what your staff members might be thinking: If meeting the expectation means that I am forced to work ten hours of overtime a week, then that may be very tough for me. Why should I do that if I cannot see why it is good for me as well? It may mean that I get a chance to keep my job, it may mean that I will get some overtime pay, or it may mean that all I get is to be tired.

"What is in it for me?" is a natural question and you must be able to answer it. Work Leaders must use the self-interest of staff members to the advantage of the organization. When individuals focus on efforts that satisfy self-interest, while at the same time supporting productive team results, the individual, the team, and the entire organization wins.

Raising the Bar

Setting expectations that raise the bar from previous performance levels is an essential part of achieving Peak

Performance. Seldom have organizations reached the highest level of success with complacency. The level of performance that is viewed as peak performance is not achieved by holding on to existing success. Peak performance is only possible when the work leader reaches. No organization can survive if it attempts to maintain the status quo. Work Leaders must constantly be looking for opportunities to "raise the bar."

At the same time, as Joe Batten says, "No team ever finishes ahead of its leader. A true responsive leader must dare to stand out from the crowd."[15] Work leaders must set the bar high and must always be striving to increase their own achievement. Leaders cannot set an example that is weak or easy. It is up to you to set the bar high for yourself as well.

These efforts must be focused on challenging associates to stretch to that next level, which is just slightly higher. Incremental improvement is the only useful approach. One small step achieved encourages another. On the other hand, pushing too hard and reaching too high can create frustration and new barriers to achievement. Balance is crucial.

How *Not* to Raise the Bar

The following exchange between a work leader and an associate illustrates the pain that results from trying to raise the bar too much and too fast. Once you go too far, the resistance can get so severe that almost anything you say can be countered with a refusal to try. Ask for too much and you may get nothing.

WORK LEADER: I have set a new expectation of our productivity standard for a processor from ten files a day to twenty-five.

ASSOCIATE: We have done ten for the last five years, how is that increase possible?

WORK LEADER: We have a new process that we believe will help increase productivity.

ASSOCIATE: Then why change it now before we know about the process?

WORK LEADER: I want to provide you with a new challenge so that we can take advantage of the gains.

ASSOCIATE: Why should I increase output by that much?

WORK LEADER: Because the company needs to increase its productivity.

ASSOCIATE: Why do I care about that?

WORK LEADER: Company profits will make us all better off.

ASSOCIATE: How?

WORK LEADER: We will make more money and there will be more money in profit sharing.

ASSOCIATE: I am not eligible for profit sharing.

WORK LEADER: You will be.

ASSOCIATE: Yes, but not now. What is in it for me today?

WORK LEADER: You get a chance to hit a new goal. The fun of being better is a good reason.

ASSOCIATE: Are you cutting staff and just trying to get me to pick up the slack?

WORK LEADER: No, but we will be able to take on more work with the same staff.

ASSOCIATE: What if we do not get any more work, are you going to cut staff then?

WORK LEADER: We are confident that we will be able to get the greater volumes.

ASSOCIATE: Are you going to pay me more?

WORK LEADER: No, not right now. Meet the new expectations, and you will be more eligible for promotion.

ASSOCIATE: What kind of promotion?

WORK LEADER: I have none specifically in mind right now.

ASSOCIATE: Are you going to pay me more money?

WORK LEADER: Not right away. Maybe, if you meet new expectations.

ASSOCIATE: Maybe? Are you kidding?

The task of setting expectations is not without its risks. Goals are designed to bring about a new course. Seldom does a new direction come easily. As Nicolo Machiavelli said in *The Prince*, "It must be considered that there is nothing more difficult to carry out nor more doubtful of success, nor more dangerous to handle than to initiate a new order of things."[16] It is essential to stay focused and to always keep the reasons for the expectations clearly in mind since the path will not be easy. Peak Performance never is.

CASE STUDY

"Kim, I am very concerned about our division's sales," said Carol. "We have been falling well behind and I think that your performance is having a serious impact on the team as a whole. What are you going to do to pick up the pace?"

Kim sat in complete silence for thirty seconds. Finally she said, "I don't understand. I have been on my personal plan for the entire year. How you can suggest that I am the one failing? I'm probably the only one who is going to exceed my previous year actual sales."

Carol was stunned. Kim's sales were good but her 10 percent increase simply was not going to be enough. "You know that the plan for this year calls for a 20 percent increase."

"I told you last December that I could not do 20 percent. In fact, I thought the best I could do was 5 percent, but I committed to 10 percent because I wanted to show you I would really push myself. I never committed to anything like 20 percent."

"I know you wanted the goal to be 10 percent," said Carol, "but top management said it needed to be 20 *percent, and that is what I committed to. I cannot have a shortfall."*

"How can you tell me, halfway through the year, that my goal is a 20 percent increase? You never told me that. I am very confused and frankly, angry. I cannot get 20 percent, and you should have known that and told top management. Also, I happen to know that no other salesperson in the division has a goal of anything close to 20 percent."

Questions

1. Why did Kim fail when she felt she was succeeding?

2. What should Carol have done to make certain that Kim was a success?

3. Could Kim succeed on her own?

4. If Carol had made certain that Kim had a clear understanding of her expectations, would Carol have been responsible for Kim's failure?

5. Kim is a "successful failure." Whose fault is that?

6. If you were Kim's boss, what would you have done differently?

7. Have you ever been in the situation Kim finds herself in? What did you do?

8. Have you ever made the same mistake that Carol made? If so, what would you do now?

CHAPTER THREE

Assignment
Square Pegs in Round Holes
Never Fit!

Setting expectations lays the groundwork for leading an organization, but having the staff to do the work is essential to getting the job done. In chapter 1, we concluded that love was the emotional and intellectual basis for effective leadership. In chapter 2, we discussed the need to set expectations and focus on the few key components that make up goal setting and action planning. Here, we turn to the people who are going to meet the expectations.

Once you know what needs to be done, you need to be certain you focus on assignment. Assignment is more complex than putting the right person in the right job. The task requires some homework before you can make these critical decisions.

WORK LEADERS TIP   How To Find The Best

One of the great challenges in assigning great people is finding them. You cannot pick great hires if you do not have great candidates. Here are some ideas that should help:

- *Make friends with your in-house recruiter.*
- *Talk to your staff. The best staff prospects can come from friends of your best staff.*
- *Look for people you encounter in retail shops who give you good service.*
- *Talk to your friends about people they know.*
- *Ask people in your family about their friends, but do not hire family members.*
- *Talk to acquaintances from your church, synagogue, or mosque. Their values may be similar to yours.*
- *Ask people you know from service clubs like Rotary and Lions Club.*
- *Join the chamber of commerce in your local area; go to the networking meetings.*
- *If you get an interesting résumé, interview the person even if you have no opening.*
- *Look at everybody you meet as a potential associate. In short, you should always be recruiting.*

You need to find people who have the same values, abilities, performance, and attitudes that you want from your best associate. If you compromise on the quality of your hires, the team will have too many weak people to win the competitive race to excellence. Assigning great people requires discipline and commitment. It also means making tough decisions when a candidate does not measure up. Pick the very best you can find! Nothing is more disastrous to an organization than hiring people who do not measure up. Many times leaders decide that they have a vacancy that must be filled and they fill it as quickly as possible. This hiring practice is almost guaranteed to result in a new hire who is fired or quits sometime soon after. Never hire just to fill a job. Learn to fill those jobs with people who are as good as, or better than, your current staff.

The case for filling jobs with the right people was never better made than by Jim Collins in his latest book, *Good to Great*. His analogy to a bus graphically contrasts the relationship between the strategic direction and the need for the right people to get the work out:

> The executives who ignited the transformations from good to great did not first figure out where to drive the bus and then get people to take it there. No, they first got the right people on the bus (and the wrong people off the bus) and then figured out where to drive it. They said, in essence, "Look, I don't really know where we should take this bus. But I know this much: If we get the right people on the bus, the right people in the right seats, and the wrong people off the bus, then we'll figure out how to take it someplace great."[17]

First Understand the Process

How do you make decisions about assignments? First, you must decide what the job or position really is and how it fits into the work process of your organization. This "systems approach" to evaluating all the jobs in your group is essential if you are to help people achieve the goals of the organization. All too often, poor leaders forget that although the end result is essential, the process determines success. For example, a boss who says, "I do not care how you do it, get the backlog out by tomorrow" gives associates great freedom, indeed, license, to do whatever they think necessary to take care of the backlog. However, since the instruction makes no reference to the quality of the work, it leaves the associates with far too much freedom to cut corners and to ignore the impact on the unit's other responsibilities, especially to other sections in the company.

How we get the job done does matter. If a process is designed to make each sequential element achieve specific results, then the entire process will be more likely to achieve superior results. Hence, it does matter what the elements are in the system. Leaders must know those elements and must continue to improve on their achievement. In short, in order to assign a task, leaders must know if the task is required, why it is required, and what defines effective

47

completion. Lastly, they must know why that accomplishment is essential to the mission of the organization.

Ironically, for many leaders, this first step in focusing on assignment is completely missed. Perhaps it is because the leader's boss said something like, "Do not mess with the system. We have worked for years to get a stable system, and we do not want you to change anything." This situation is not unusual. Inertia is a terrible disease in many organizations.

Other leaders fail to look into the process because it takes so long to do it right or because it is hard work. Much to their chagrin, eventually the cost of avoidance exceeds the cost of commitment.

Whatever the case, leaders must develop a clear knowledge, not just of the process and the jobs within it, but of how their part of the process affect others in the organization. What one associate does will have an influence on the others; similarly what one unit does will have an influence on the other units in an organization. Your unit must be linked through an effective process to the rest of the organization. Your output must meet the demands of the customer or of other units in the firm. The recipient of your finished product or service is either an external or an internal customer. Be certain the customer gets what is desired and required.

If the process you manage is not functioning properly, if it does not produce the intended result effectively, then it requires mending. A broken process can destroy an organization, but it can also destroy an individual assigned to it. Before you make an assignment, consider the human result of failure created by a work process that makes success impossible for any incumbent. Once again, make these decisions with love in mind.

Look at the Job Description

Why create a job description? The staff knows what to do, why waste the time? This is the classic argument against the disciplined effort to organize job requirements. Henry Mintzberg in his classic book on organization made the case for a disciplined process and structure so as to make certain that every staff member knows what to do.

Standardization of work content is a very tight coordinating mechanism. Firemen cannot stop each time they arrive at a fire to figure out who will attach the hose to the hydrant and who will go up the ladder; similarly, airline pilots must be sure about their landing procedures well in advance of descent.[18]

Once the system or process is understood and once you have determined that the process is the correct process, then you, the leader, must know and understand the components of the jobs. For each job, you need to ask questions like

- What actually must be done by the person?

- Is the work manual or is it a "knowledge worker" job that requires more to be done in the head than with the hands?

- What are the working hours of the job?

- When is the output required?

- How much am I permitted to pay for the right person?

- Where does the person need to work: at home or in the office?

- Is there specific knowledge required?

- Are there special skills required?

The list goes on and on. This job definition task is generally made easier if the organization has made the commitment to write a position description. However, even with a job description, you will probably need to ask many critical questions about each job. Job descriptions have a way of becoming out of date almost the first month after they are written. They may not represent reality even when they are brand new. Only you as the leader can determine what the real job requirements are.

You may have no previous knowledge or experience with the jobs you need to assign. Whether they are vacant or not, you still must evaluate the jobs for the specific duties and for performance requirements. This may be more important when the jobs are filled than when they are vacant. A job filled by the wrong person, doing the wrong tasks, can be more of a problem than one not filled at all. Each leader must look at each job and understand the nature and requirements of the job. If you are blessed with a great performer in a job, then make certain that you can be sure that the incumbent is doing what the job description says should be the job tasks. Frequently, a great performer will be performing tasks that are not in the job description or doing them very differently from the job description.

Many jobs are created by the person filling them. When we replace a person, we may find the newcomer is failing because the newcomer is only doing the job in the job description, not the job that her predecessor was actually doing. If new associates have this problem, their salvation could be to find the old incumbent. If that is impossible, then they, and you, may need to go back to the process and find out how this job fits into the "bigger picture." This type of exercise should never be foisted on a new associate. It is the Work Leader's duty to resolve the confusion long before the new associate arrives. If you cannot do that, then at least you will need to give the newcomer some time and understanding until you both can redefine the job.

Writing a Useful Job Description

Almost every organization has a job description system; however, at times new jobs have not been formally documented. If you have not been provided with a description for a job that falls within your authority, you may have an advantage if you actually fill the void with your version of the job description.

If you are going to be creating a job description, here are some simple steps you can follow to make certain that the candidate and you have a clear understanding of what the job is. In addition, this job description assumes that you will take those expectations you laid out earlier and translate them into clear criteria that will be used to ultimately make a judgment on performance. It is as simple as *A, B, C.*

A.   Define Expectations

Start first with defining the results required of the job. This takes us back to the expectations we talked about in the previous chapter. You must carefully define what success on the job really means for the associate and the organization. If the job is to process applications for a loan, then what does a "processed loan" mean? What should it look like? How will you know it is done well? What is the expected quality of the paperwork? How many loans should be accomplished in a day? In short, define the outputs of the job.

B.   Process

Once you have done the expectations, *then* you must specify how that job gets done. It may be the way it was done before you had the opening, or it may be a new way. Do this in a detailed manner so that you can use it as a training document for the new individual as well. If you know how to draw a flow chart, make one. If you are more comfortable with a step-by-step list of the actions required, do that. Since few jobs have only one task that the person must do, you will need to make a list for each element of the job. Make certain that it defines clearly what the person will be doing each and every day.

C.   Requirements

Now define what it takes to be able to do this job. Here you should write down the criteria (knowledge, skills, and attitudes) that the applicant must have in order to be successful. If the person needs to be good at numbers and must be skilled in operating a calculator, then make that clear. If the associate needs no previous knowledge of processing loans, then make that clear as well. In every respect, be very specific about the core requirements any candidate must have in order to be successful.

The Requirements of the Job Versus the Abilities of the Person

Knowing what must be done is only the first step. Knowing what it takes to do a job is the second. The whole process of assigning people to tasks really turns on your ability to pick people with the ability to succeed. Those who have the knowledge, skills, and attitudes to do the tasks involved in the job will succeed; those without them will fail. People may be able to refine their knowledge and skills on the job, but if they come with significant shortages, you will wait a long time for them to meet your expectations. In fact, they may fail first. Richard Fear in his book *The Evaluation Interview* says, "All too many people have been placed in positions that, on the one hand, make relatively little use of their real aptitudes and interests and, on the other hand, make demands upon them in areas where they are the weakest."[19] How right he is.

The same is even truer about attitudes. It's not that you cannot change attitudes, but the journey from weak and negative attitudes to good, strong and positive attitudes is painful, stressful, and uncertain. Do not waste your time being a social worker when it comes to attitude. If a candidate reflects a negative attitude, then move on. Life as a leader is already a challenge; don't add to it by trying to be a psychotherapist. We will focus more on this when we discuss development and evaluation.

How do you determine what the key characteristics of a successful candidate for a job might be? Start with the functions in the job. If the job calls for somebody to talk to customers and ask them for personal information, then it is essential that the candidate have good communications skills, a capacity for sincerity, and a sensitivity to people's anxieties. If a candidate lacks interpersonal skills or seems introverted, you need to consider another person for the role. If the role requires strong financial analysis skills, then a person with no accounting background and without a strong systematic thought process would probably be a failure.

Job assignment is the process of matching job requirements with personal abilities. A mismatch is almost always a prescription for disaster. Certainly some shortcomings may be corrected remedially, but if the core capabilities for accomplishing the job tasks are missing, both you and the candidate will be unsuccessful and unhappy. Do not set candidates up for failure just because you think they are good people. Although positive attitudes are essential, they are not sufficient. Good attitudes can make up for many weaknesses, but they cannot make up for a lack of capabilities.

Skills and core personal competencies matter. Personal characteristics vary greatly, and some of them can be critical to success. Such characteristics may be obvious to all interested parties; others may not. Some examples of what to look for might be:

- Candidates for an accounting clerk assignment who pay attention to detail and have basic arithmetic skills

- Machinist candidates with have steady hands

- Purchasing clerks candidates with strong verbal skills and the ability to deal with a broad range of vendor personnel who might be inclined to sell hard

- Candidates for customer service representative who can patiently receive insults from irate customers

- Bank teller candidates who can add and subtract and have a pleasant demeanor when under stress

- Candidates for systems analyst who have logical, structured thinking skills.

Many of these may seem obvious to some and surprising to others. It is essential that the work leader knows and understands how these types of personal characteristics might impact success in any given job.

Once again, Jim Collins makes the point, "It all starts with disciplined people. The transition begins not by trying to discipline the wrong people into the right behaviors, but by getting self-disciplined people on the bus in the first place."[20] Make certain candidates have the right skills and the right attitudes and you have a much better chance of achieving Peak Performance.

WORK LEADERS TIP How Do You Look for the Right Qualities in a Candidate?

There is no foolproof way to make the right hiring decision. The key is to focus on what really matters, not on questions that are easy to answer.

Do not ask questions that

- *Can be answered by reading a résúme or by doing reference checks*

- *Are illegal by virtue of federal or state statute*

- *Pose political, philosophical, or religious issues*

- *Are personal and have nothing to do with how that candidate will do in the work environment*

- *Have nothing to do with the candidate's ability or interest in doing the job*

Do ask questions that

- *Help you understand what the person has really done in previous jobs, such as, "What were your duties?"*

- *Ask the applicant about actions taken under specific circumstances, for example, "What did you do when...?"*

- *Reveal accomplishments and how they were measured, such as, "What were the results of...?"*

- *Cause the person to show problem-solving skills, such as, "How would you handle...?"*

- *Prove the candidate's general interests and goals, such as, "What is your career goal in five years?"*

- *Probe the candidate's self-awareness, such as, "What are the things you do best? Worst?"*

Strong Résúmes and Weak Interviews

You should not interview a candidate whose résúme fails to pass the essential criteria test. Once you have established a job's key criteria for education, experience, and results you should not waver in your commitment to finding a candidate having those characteristics. These résúme essentials are obviously only proxies for the true measure of someone's knowledge and skills, but they are critical. A candidate is seldom going to look better than what you see on a carefully crafted résúme. Compromise at this point is almost certainly going to lower the bar you have established for the initial filtering process. Keep your expectations high. Do not waste your time on candidates who simply do not meet the minimum requirements of the job. Even in the tightest of labor markets, capable people are available, and you need to use your time to recruit them.

One useful technique is to carefully review candidate résúmes during the initial sorting process, pick those that have the best apparent qualifications, make a short list of candidates to interview, and then put the résúmes aside. When the time for a candidate interview comes, avoid rereading the résúme prior to the interview and concentrate your energy on the interview. This focuses your attention on interviewing the person, not the résúme. Obviously a candidate can mislead or even lie on a résúme; hence, some part of your interview will always be dedicated to pursuing areas that you did not fully understand on the résúme as well as areas that might be an opportunity for misstatement or misperception. A résúme can provide a chronology of a candidate's working career, but it can also get in the way of understanding the real essence of the work experience and accomplishments and, perhaps, prevent key insights into the person's knowledge, skills, attitudes, and behaviors.

Résúmes tell you what candidate's did, and seldom indicate clearly how and how well they accomplished the successes they offer. As an example, if a candidate worked for five years as an accounts payable clerk, you really need to know what she did, how her success was measured, and how she achieved success. It is essential that you understand how those criteria fit your expectations of the job you are

55

discussing with the candidate. As another example, what if you are hiring a hair stylist? How did her customers view her performance? How did the stylist generate new customers? What was the stylist's productivity? If you are hiring a lawyer, what is the best way to determine the person's research capability? How can you know what the client satisfaction was? Is the attorney capable of sound analysis that is efficiently completed? Is the cost of an opinion more than can be charged to a client?

Prior behavior is a great predictor of future behavior, so do not let yourself think that a person will change. What you are looking for are behaviors that will help that individual to be successful. You are also looking for people who have demonstrated success as required by the employer. It is essential to make certain that those successes will match your expectations of the knowledge, skills, and attitudes that are required for your job. You are not doing social work. You want winners, so look for them and then hire them.

A résúme is a statement by a candidate of what he or she thinks you want to know or should know. Sometimes that effort is successful, and many times it is not. Your goal as interviewer must be to determine the insights that you believe are critical to making a judgment about the candidate's ability to fill your needs. Short of mind reading, you have no better way of understanding the candidate's fit with your organization than to spend time probing the candidate's history of accomplishments, learning, and growth potential. That is why the interview really is the most valuable assignment tool you have at your disposal. This applies for internal candidates as well as external. You must always do a legitimate and thorough interview of all candidates, even those you work with every day. Familiarity is no reason to forgo your opportunity to interview candidates.

A résúme is a wealth of information, but the interview will be the key to your discovery. Andy Grove, in *High Output Management* sums it up, "The purpose of an interview is to: Select a good performer, educate him as to who you and the company are, determine if a mutual match exists, and sell him on the job."[21]

Close Your Mouth, Open Your Mind

The most serious mistake in the interview process is for an interviewer to do all of the talking. Indeed, the best interviews are those where the candidate speaks 95 percent of the time or more. "Active listening," a term coined by psychologist Dr. Carl Rogers, is the key to a quality interview. Obviously, the questions are important, but the more critical aspect is the answers. Once you understand an answer, it can often lead to another question that probes a bit further. If you are speaking, then it is very difficult for you to be listening. Unfortunately, all too often when people are listening, they are probably listening to themselves. You already know about yourself. Your goal must be to learn about the candidate.

Close your mouth, open your ears, engage your brain, and then ask a question. Listen to the response, process the answer, and then ask follow-up questions. That is the sequence of activity required for active listening. If you do anything else, you are interviewing yourself. Never underestimate the value of follow-up questions. Do not accept a candidate's "sound bite." You must focus on the details of the answer and on getting both a broad and a deep understanding of how the candidate succeeded in previous work environments. Ask open-ended questions that require real answers from real experiences. Ask questions like, "Give me an example of how you managed your worst customer problem." Or, "Tell me about the time you spent at Mega Corporation as a financial analyst" or, "Tell me about your first job and how you liked your first boss."

Vague questions will get vague answers. Never ask a question that allows a candidate to give a theoretical or conceptual answer unless you are looking for critical thinking skills. Questions like, "What is a good employee?" may be good at getting an intellectual insight into employee management but will not give you specific insights into a candidate's behavior. Instead you might try, "When you last had a fellow associate who was not getting the job done effectively and was getting you and your unit into difficulty with management, how did you handle the problem?" What you want are answers as to what candidates have actually done and how they achieved results. Remember, you are looking for winners, and the only way to find them is to probe for their successes and how they achieved them.

In chapter 1, we described the differences between love and like. This message carries over throughout this book, and it has direct application in the interview. You cannot afford to like a candidate. You must always be on guard against strongly liking a résumé before you have the opportunity to interview a candidate. It is very easy to say this but much harder to do. You must enter an interview with an open mind.

Just as importantly, you must not allow yourself to be influenced by liking a candidate during your interview. This is even harder. We all have had the experience of meeting a person and, within seconds, feeling a "chemistry" with that person that seems to establish a bond. Remember you are hiring the whole person. Liking a candidate can severely constrain the objectivity you need to determine the fit of the individual for the specific job, the team, or the corporate world. Certainly, if the chemistry is bad, it may portend a relationship problem in the future, but good chemistry is not a predictor of high-quality job performance. In fact, strong positive chemistry frequently has an adverse impact on a leader's ability to effectively manage an associate. You probably should avoid hiring people you do not like, but do not simply hire all candidates you like. Hire those you love because they are humans. Hire those who, through past experiences, have demonstrated that they have the knowledge, skills, attitudes, and behaviors they need to help you achieve great results for the organization. Any other reasons should fall way down the list of selection criteria.

WORK LEADERS **TIP**

Control Everything
About the Interview

Most Work Leaders try hard to not appear to be a "controlling personality," and that may usually be a good objective. In an interview, it is not. You must not allow an applicant to control the interview. This is your time to make a judgment about the applicant and you need to be on your agenda, not his. Do it with courtesy, but make certain you cover your ground.

- *Make certain that you have the interview location set up well in advance. Be organized.*

- *Take applicants to the location and direct their movement. You lead the way.*

- *Have the environment match your leadership style—informal or formal.*

- *Tell applicants you will be asking a number of questions first. Their questions come at the end.*

- *Prepare a list of questions that you are going to ask, and ask them.*

- *Always get an answer to your questions.*

- *Bore deep—get to the details.*

- *Focus on listening to the answers. Never let a question go by without a follow-up question.*

- *Probe behaviors and work experiences. Ask what they did, not how they felt.*

- *If you pose hypothetical questions, let them have time to think, but not too long.*

- *Tie your questions to their résumé. Get examples of what they did, how it worked, and why.*

Hiring from Within

Entering the ranks of leader will quickly put you into the business of assigning staff. If you already have people working for you, when a vacancy comes up in your organization, the natural tendency is to fill the job from within. Promoting from within has all of the obvious benefits of offering growth opportunities to existing staff while at the same time allowing you to deal with people you know. Looking outside your own section or department to elsewhere in the organization usually will provide you with a staff member that is better known and understood than from someone outside the organization; however, your lack of personal knowledge will still exist. Eventually, you will be relying on an "internal reference." Since the primary reference will probably be a former boss, you can expect the internal sources to be more candid than an external source. Obviously you should also look to other staff members in the organization to help, including the human resources department. Management personnel who have solid objectivity and sound evaluation skills can be very helpful, but you must refine your own interviewing skills so that you can make your own judgments as well.

Keep in mind that there are also risks to the approach of hiring internally. Some of your staff may be falling short of your expectations. If that is the case, reassigning them is like moving the deck chairs on the *Titanic*, and it will not save the sinking ship nor will it help the organization as a whole. Make certain you are not getting another leader's failures. In addition, the fact that an internal candidate is doing a good job in a current assignment could bias your view on the new opportunity. Make the judgment based on the job skills you have concluded are critical for success in your job and not on how a candidate has done in another job.

Weak performers cannot be accepted in the long run. If you have internal candidates who have demonstrated the capacity to achieve mediocrity, then you need to consider the merits of new blood. New, aggressive talent added to an established team of slow and mediocre performers can energize the entire team. The impact of new energy can cause a team to find a new life and a new vitality. Of course, the new team member may also be influenced by the lethargic old team and become mediocre, but it is less likely.

Don't Roll the Dice, Luck Is Against You!

How many times have you said, "I really am not happy with this candidate, but I need someone to fill the job, so I am going to roll the dice on this one"? How many times was that a good choice? Probably, if you are truly honest with yourself, the answer will be, "Almost never."

That should be all that is needed to make the point, but it is not. Every manager has made such a bad decision, and unfortunately, most will make it again. Why? The answer is simple: desperation and maybe even a little panic. No advice from this chapter can have a more immediate impact on your success than this: avoid quick fixes in staffing. You would be better off hiring a temporary employee during the time that it takes to find a permanent replacement, rather than hire the wrong candidate. The negative impact of a bad apple on unit morale and organizational achievement can be so severe that the recovery time will far exceed the delay in hiring the right person. Live with the pain in the short run, and avoid the much greater agony of picking the wrong person who ultimately must be fired. Use care and don't take a chance on an obvious misfit.

61

Assigning a new hire to any job in your organization can seem like a gamble, but you do not need to go outside the organization to find a misfit. The same type of mistake can be made when you promote a person from within the organization to the wrong job. The person, in all likelihood, is one of your better employees or you would not have taken the risk of the move. All too often, these "misplacements" have multiple costs to the organization. First, a bad placement can create an incumbent who is failing to deliver on the organizational goals. Second, you lose a good employee from the old job. Third, if the old job is vacant for an extended period, a performance drop for your unit may result. In short, your roll of the dice may create more problems than it solves.

A bad placement can negatively affect organizational achievement. The leader also suffers from the misplacement, because the staff will recognize the error and ultimately the leader's credibility will be challenged. The concern is not for your wounded ego but rather for the impact your credibility has on your staff. All associates in an organization want to have confidence in their leader. When you are a new leader, your staff will start out with a relatively unblemished opinion of your ability to lead. Each error you make demonstrates your humanness; however, too many errors will not be viewed as human frailty but begin to look more like ineffectiveness. Of course, no leader can function without errors; however, no leader can afford to make too many mistakes before the staff begins to question her ability to lead.

Your people selection skills will get the first and most serious scrutiny, because they will speak volumes about how you view people and what you expect of the staff. If you think that your staff will not notice, think again. Like it or not, as a leader you are always on stage. Every action you take will be evaluated as an indication of your ability. The good news is that if you, on balance, make more good decisions than bad, you are likely to be viewed favorably. The bad news is that you will be judged most harshly on actions that reflect how you feel about people. If your actions in selection and assignment reflect an inability to choose quality people, or people who have the requisite knowledge, skills, and attitudes to deliver on the organization's objectives, then you will lose your following.

Unfortunately, the promoted associate is the person most seriously damaged when we make an assignment error. Having taken a good performer and provided the exhilaration of a promotion, we then have put her through the agony of feeling inadequate as she comes to recognize that the new job is a bad fit. In a rather brief time, we put this quality person on an emotional roller-coaster and turned a winner into a failure.

This is nothing short of a human crisis for the associate. Now is when love is needed. First, you must recognize the problem quickly, decide if it is a failed assignment, and, if so, reverse the decision quickly. Second, you need to find a way to help the person recover by providing an opportunity for a positive performance experience. Find that person another job that uses her skills rather than her weaknesses. This may be in your organization or it may be in another, but do it quickly. Self-esteem is fragile, and your ability to act quickly will reflect your sincere love for the individual and can help to rekindle confidence and a feeling of self-worth. Failure to act appropriately is most certainly going to cause the individual to not only lose self-esteem but also to look for a way to avoid the embarrassment of facing peers who witnessed the failure.

Unless you intervene, the associate is likely to be a casualty to both herself and a major loss to the organization. On the other hand, if you have a great fit, then your associate will love the job, and so will you.

Find the Stars

The simple truth about staffing is that if you staff with mediocrity, you will get average performance. If you staff with stars, you will soar, and peak performance will follow. There is no substitute for stars. Organizations with winning performance records have a disproportionate number of stars on the staff. You can too, but it takes discipline and a commitment to never accept average performance when choosing staff. If you want to be a winner, you need to focus on hiring winners. Loyalty to average performers may be honorable, but it is unlikely to create a winning organization. You must love your quality associates enough to make certain that the people who weaken the performance of the team are moved out. We need to love each staff member but not to the exclusion or the detriment of peak performance. You must love your team enough to assign only the best.

Unfortunately, we all have a tendency to get comfortable with average performance. When somebody is meeting expectations, we normally are pleased, yet we should always be striving to improve the existing level of performance. Good enough is *not* good enough. General Electric did not get to be the winner it is by accepting average performance. Toyota did not get to be the quality leader in automobile manufacturing by accepting good-enough cars. Your company or your section cannot excel if its goal is to be average, and that is what you communicate to the staff when you accept average performance.

Every group of staff members will have a person who represents the best and another person who represents the worst in the group. Even if you think a group overall is above average in performance, somebody is always lagging. The two lessons here are first, keep the best performer, and second, either help the worst get much better or help the worst leave. Is that cruel? No, it just means setting the bar where stars can make the grade and the average either strive for improvement or drop out. Group performance will attempt to rise to the level of expectations, but if the persons assigned are not of the highest quality, then that journey can be long, painful, and even frustrating. Pick the best, act like a true leader for them, and the staff will get better and better over time.

Obviously, the higher the level of stars you have, the harder it will be to hold on to their talent. That, however, does not mean you will always lose the best. Something about stars causes them to want to be around the best. Even if they have a chance to go to a big job at another company with less talent, most stars will opt—assuming you are really leading—to stay with stars like themselves rather than work in an environment that is short on energy and high on mediocrity. Build a team of stars and you will have more fun, they will have more fun, and the organization will outperform its competition. That is what stars are all about—winning.

If you are a work leader of professional staff, then the star is even more important because so much depends on their ability to be superior individual performers in their technical specialty. In their book, *Aligning the Stars*, Jay Lorsch and Tom Tierney discuss how important the star is to the professional services firm. "Outstanding firms are consistently able to identify, attract, and retain star performers; to stars committed to their firm's strategy; to manage stars across geographic distance, business lines, and generations; to govern and lead so that both the organization and its stars prosper and feel rewarded. These capabilities are what give great firms their competitive advantage."[22]

To Find Stars,
Do Not Look to the Heavens,
Look to the Ground!

The key to having a winning team is to have great players. The New York Yankees keep winning because they have stars. Of course, the Yankees' owner pays whatever it takes to get the stars, and most of us do not have that kind of budget. So what we need to do is to find the stars who do not yet think that they should be paid a star wage. We need to find a person with raw talent and then find a way to encourage that person to be an outstanding performer. In short, you need to be the talent scout who sees the greatness in a Babe Ruth before the Babe hits all those home runs. That takes lots of time and probably some luck; however, the payoff is huge.

65

Here are some qualities to look for to find the type of person who can become a star in your organization:

- *A spectacular academic track record. Intelligence and discipline matter.*

- *Evidence of the ability to work one or more jobs and go to school full time. This shows a willingness to work hard in order to achieve a goal.*

- *Great verbal skills. There is almost no job where verbal skills are unimportant.*

- *A quality résumé that focuses on measurable and quantitative results.*

- *The ability to write well. Writing well is essential in almost every job.*

- *Evidence of job change motivated by a lack of challenge. You want commitment to success.*

- *A person with demonstrated skill and accomplishment in your field. Great experience and success matter.*

- *Evidence that the candidate's expectations are based in reality but her dreams are high. People who reach and win.*

- *Behaviors that show a high energy level and enthusiasm. High energy gets the job done.*

- *Evidence that the person is not satisfied with mediocrity. This defines the star mindset.*

CASE STUDY

Sarah was about to go home when she saw her boss walking to her desk. This was not what she wanted or needed at the end of this terrible day. She knew that Barbara was going to give her another lecture about credit approval processing. Sarah did not need another reminder that she had a bad day. Almost every day had been a bad day in the six months since she took on this new job.

Barbara said, "Sarah, you turned down five more credit applications today that you should have easily approved. Honestly, I do not understand why you cannot get it. You did such a great job as an application processor. This move to credit analyst should have been a snap."

"I don't get it and that is just the point," Sarah said. "I still do not understand what I am supposed to be doing. I know you have taught me several times, and I have read the book three times. I think I understand it, but when it comes time to complete the numbers analysis, I get confused. I never was very good at math in high school, and some of this stuff I am

supposed to do is very hard for me." What Sarah could not bring herself to say was that she really hated working with all of those numbers. When she was processing applications, she loved the work. She loved talking to applicants on the phone, and she loved writing letters to them. Her new work was boring, and worse, she hated not being able to talk to clients anymore. She felt isolated and cut off from people. "If only I could get the same pay but do what I did before," she said.

"Well, I do not think that is possible, Sarah. We promoted you to your current position because we had a crisis opening and because we knew you were ambitious and would work hard to catch on. Were we wrong?"

Sarah thought for a minute and then said, "No, I will work even harder, and I will get it right!" But she knew it was not possible. That was the moment when she decided that she needed to look for a new job. This one was making her miserable. She knew the company would easily find another processor who would be willing to take the same chance she did.

67

Questions

1. Sarah is miserable. Why is she so unhappy? Could anybody have predicted the problem?

2. What should Sarah do? Is there a way out of her misery?

3. What should have been done to avoid the problem for Sarah and Barbara?

4. What should Barbara do? Can she save Sarah or is it inevitable that Sarah will leave or be fired?

CHAPTER FOUR

Development
The Good Get Better, The Best Excel!

This chapter, the midpoint of the mnemonic LEADERS, is also the central theme of our journey. Your associates rely on your commitment to them and nowhere does that commitment get tested, indeed proven, more than when you are focused on development. Your job is to commit time to developing people's abilities. Focus on development, and that gamble on a new associate becomes an investment. Fail to commit, and the gamble will frequently result in a loss. Stephen Covey makes the case this way, "The basic role of the leader is to foster mutual respect and build a complementary team where each strength is made productive and each weakness made irrelevant."[23]

The goal of a great Work Leader is to assign great people and give them room. But, "giving them room" does not mean "getting out of their way." Work Leaders cannot get out of the way, but they must give their staff an opportunity to win based on their own abilities. It is a fine line between allowing staff members to achieve success and giving them so much room that they achieve failure instead.

Think about it this way: some swimming instructors like to use natural instincts to teach children how to swim. When a young child is thrown into the pool to swim, what is likely to happen? The child may panic at first, and then most will begin to paddle doggy-style and manage to stay afloat. A small number actually continue to panic, and without help from an adult, a serious situation could develop, even drowning. No responsible adult will allow that to happen; before long, the child will be saved. You must do the same for your staff. If it becomes obvious that a staff member is drowning, you must save him.

Using the infant example further, the doggy paddle may keep a child afloat, but it is not swimming. Swimming is a skill that must be learned, generally from somebody who knows how to swim. The key skills required for success must also be learned. Talented people will find a way to survive. That, however, is not the goal. You want them to succeed, and sometimes even the strongest can drown if they do not get help.

Training and development are an investment in accomplishing the mission. By training, we usually mean the process of providing structured learning of specific subject matter. That could be knowledge, skills, or even attitudes. By development, we mean the broader scope of all those actions that are taken to facilitate the growth of an associate. That could be training, but it could also be something as simple and powerful as a comment correcting a mistake. Every interaction a work leader has with his associates should be viewed as a development action.

Psychiatrist and counselor to many executives, Dr. Harry Levinson says it this way, "Has the leader a right to mold and shape? Of what use is aging, experience, and wisdom if not to be the leaven for those who are younger? Of what use is pain if not to teach others to avoid it? The leader not only has the right; if he is leader, he has the obligation."[24]

The best outside hire in the world, the best internal promotion in the world still needs an investment in the person who is to do the work. Organizations invest in machines, computers, desks, and buildings, but all too often they make a trivial investment in the most precious factor of production, and that is people. Think about your own case. When you started either your first job or your last, did you know everything there was to know on the first day of work? Obviously, not. So what happened? If you were lucky, and worked for the right leader, you learned all about the job, perhaps even well before you started performing the required tasks. If you were even luckier, you learned from the leader each day on the job. If not, you made lots of mistakes and, with some persistence, eventually learned enough to get by. Had the company made an investment in you, you would have been more productive faster.

Development is hard work, and it requires a commitment to take the time and spend the money and a belief that a better trained and developed associate is a better performer. Once again, love for the individual persists as the driving force. If you really love your associates, you will give the time to train them so that they can learn to be more effective. This is good not only for the organization but also for them. No associate wants to fail; however, few will truly succeed if we do not help them develop.

Most development begins with some type of training session for new associates. Some companies commit a large amount of money and time to formal training classes, usually taught by full time staff and conducted in formal class settings. These sessions typically are designed to teach technical skills for a specific job and frequently give a general background on the company and its business practices as well. A new employee who is given this type of training is fortunate that his company believes in training and has committed resources to that end.

On the other hand, many companies provide training to newly assigned staff through on-the-job training (OJT). In this case, the training function is held by the organizational leader or management and the training becomes a part of the day-to-day work flow. Most people who enter new jobs get most of their training through OJT. Proponents of OJT argue that the company saves the cost of a big training department. At the same time, new staff members learn from the people who really know how to do the work. Critics argue that too many people who are trained this way do not learn anything but the practices, even errors, of the workers in the field.

WORK LEADERS TIP

Use Formal Training in Even the Smallest Unit

An organization, whatever its size, will have some type of formal training experience for new associates. It may be an orientation program, technical training, sales training, or even management training.

Should a Work Leader have a formal training program in his unit? The answer is yes, since a failure to formalize training often suggests that it is unimportant. We have a tendency to formalize those actions that we think are important. We tend to do tasks informally when we think we may never be required to do them again. When it comes to training, any perception that a new associate will never again be required to act in the manner being taught is dangerous, naïve, and foolish. You will train again, and, when you do, you will probably be doing the same training all over again for the next new associate. That suggests structure and, therefore, formality.

Formal does not necessarily mean in a classroom, but you should have a preplanned program, a set schedule of events and time frames for the training, a deadline for completion, a set of specific learning outcomes, and a way of assessing if the learning has occurred. Testing is the most common way to accomplish assessment.

Some hints for a successful training program include these:

- *Where possible, the Work Leader should be the trainer. Your success is on the line.*

- *If you assign the training to another associate, be certain it is somebody who likes doing it.*

- *If you assign the training to another associate, make certain he is good at it.*

- *Provide the new associate with a copy of the entire schedule. Emphasize planning early.*

- *Explain what the expectations are for the associate's learning. Put emphasis on our* **E.**

- *Use the three-step rule. You want them to remember what they learned so repeat, repeat!*

  1. Tell them what you will teach them.

  2. Teach them.

  3. Tell them what you taught them.

- *Teach the concepts first, then the detail. They need to know why and what.*

- *Test learning, reward success. If something is not learned, teach it again, only differently.*

- *Have the associate teach you what he learned—great way to test knowledge.*

- *Use lots of examples and practical exercises. You are not teaching theory; you want results!*

73

OJT Doesn't Mean *Omit* the Job Training

You report to your new job and you find out that your training will be right at the job site, not in a classroom. You are excited about learning the new job, especially when you are told that your trainer, Sally, is the most qualified processor in the division. Now you will be trained by the best. Sally, it turns out, is the woman in the corner with all of those stacks of files on her desk. You go over to introduce yourself and you find out that Sally is very busy and will get to you just as soon as she finishes her critical processing. After what seems like a very long time, you begin to realize that everything on Sally's desk is critical processing and that you are going to be on your own for a while.

So goes the experience of most people promised OJT. They start a new job with the promise of full training, only to find out that they are going to receive on-the-job training.

Six weeks later, they find out that in their organization, OJT means *omit* job training. What a tragedy. Not only have the expectations of a new employee been built up and let down, but the new employee probably is forced to learn most of the tasks required on his own. Picking up a little information here and a little there, the new associate spends a great deal of time trying to sort out what is correct and what is just confusion on somebody's part. This clearly wastes a great deal of the new associate's time, but worse still, the rest of the staff is distracted with a barrage of questions— more wasted time. Further, the department probably has huge amounts of rework, correcting the mistakes made by the new associate. If the new associate is unlucky enough, the boss will come around and conclude that this new player is a slow learner or a low-potential associate.

Does the training mandate by your organization include an on-the-job component? Are you responsible for accomplishing that OJT program? Has everybody in your unit received the required training? If OJT is not a required part of the organization, when was the last time you trained a new associate on the job? Did you make a plan and stick to it? Was it effective? Did the program actually help that associate grow into the job? All of these questions are critical because they focus on your responsibility as a developer. You cannot ignore the critical role you play in the development of your associates, and OJT is the key in many organizations to the successful development of its associates.

Of course, OJT can be a very effective process for training a new person. With good planning and disciplined follow-up, the process probably is more meaningful for the new associate and more cost effective for the organization. OJT is a great way to learn. When an organization takes an outstanding performer and makes that person a true mentor and encourages a real commitment of time, training a new associate will provide the kind of quality experience that can provide for a great start. Mentors need to be enthusiastic about the mentoring, and they must also fully understand the policies, practices, and procedures of the organization as well as the specific job. Further, mentoring requires patience and, yes, love to be effective. Mentors must truly want to help the person learn and be willing to share knowledge. Not all experts are so inclined, but if a mentor is sincere, then the process will work, and work very well.

Problems come when mentors lack any of these characteristics, and unfortunately, failure is more the rule than the exception. Leaders must be committed to the concept of training. However, the need to get the work out often drives them to neglect effective training. The end result usually is that the work gets out today, the crisis continues tomorrow, and the training never happens. Hence, the crisis goes on indefinitely.

There is never any easy or convenient time for training and development, yet it is a must if you are to be an effective leader. Dr. Thomas Gordon says:

> Leaders do a lot of teaching—giving instructions, explaining new policies or procedures, doing on-the-job training. Yet very few leaders have received special training to carry out this important function. They don't appreciate how difficult it is to teach people effectively—it is more complex than most people think.
>
> In the first place, it is not commonly understood how much people resist being placed in the position of having to learn something new. It's hard work because it requires giving up accustomed ways of doing things and familiar ways of thinking about things. Learning requires change, and change can be disturbing—even threatening at times. Besides, the role of "a learner" in relation to "a teacher" is often felt as demeaning, no doubt because all of us remember being put down, punished, and patronized in school by our teachers. This means that when leaders teach, they must avoid using teaching methods that will make their subordinates feel they're being treated like children.[25]

How you structure the training is critical. The training must be focused on what it takes to be successful. Each training experience must be tailored to the current level of competence in the individual being trained. As difficult as it may be, you must learn what the new associate really knows. Once you have a good sense of the associate's level of knowledge and skill, then you can address the second area of focus. Do you have a list of all the required knowledge, skills, and attitudes that will make each person a fully capable performer? If not, make a list of those and take the time to check with your associates to find out if you have missed anything.

Now you are ready to design an effective OJT experience. Without those first two steps, you will lose the advantage of OJT tailored to the individual. At this point, preparing a plan for each person not fully skilled will be easy and effective. Make certain it is structured along the needs and skills defined and make certain that you are able to validate the learning. This usually means that you are continuously testing the knowledge being absorbed. These can be formal tests or that can be informal questions asked during the training. You must know if the associate is learning.

WORK LEADERS TIP — Have You Made These OJT Mistakes?

In spite of the potential positives, many pitfalls can make OJT a disaster. Watch out for statements like these or the result will be a poorly trained associate, probably also with an attitude problem.

- *"Here is the Operations Manual. Read this and come back in three days."*

- *"I do not have time for you today. Go home and come back tomorrow."*

- *"I just showed you the basics. Now go and read the manual to understand the details."*

- *"This manual is all wrong. We do it differently."*

- *"I know what the corporate policy is, but we changed our procedures. Don't tell corporate."*

- *"Here is a stack of work. Go give it a try."*

- *"I do not know how to do that, but we can figure it out later."*
- *"I know that is what Frank said to do, but it is not important enough to do every time."*
- *"I hate this job and I cannot believe that you will like it either."*
- *"We did half of today's training, let's just quit and get back to it tomorrow."*
- *"I hate training people. I would rather be doing my own job."*

Classroom Training:
You're Teaching Adults, Not School Children

At some point, a new associate will probably endure some type of formal classroom training. Although we have said OJT is very productive, it is also true that at times the nature of the training demands a more intense, disciplined, and controlled environment. A classroom gives the trainer substantial control over the subject matter shared. It provides for the use of professional teaching tools and techniques and allows the organization to be certain that all of the associates are experiencing the same learning outcomes. This is particularly important when the subject matter is complex. Also, by controlling the environment, a trainer can increase the efficiency of the learning experience by avoiding the inevitable distractions of getting the work out.

Does your organization have a formal training program for new staff members? Has every staff member in your unit been through that program? If not, why not? If it is because you have failed to get them there because the work load keeps you from releasing them, you are not doing your job. No matter how effective your OJT has been, getting your associates trained in the formal process will be critical to their success.

If you are doing the training, remember that these are adults in the classroom. Adult learners are more impatient with a classroom environment, more challenging of a teacher, more inflexible in their receptivity to new knowledge, and more eager for real-world applicability rather than conceptual background.

Adults have the benefit, and the burden, of life experience. This is why they react the way they do in a classroom. Most have completed all of the formal education they intend to experience. They have added to that learning a set of life experiences that have shaped their frame of reference. For example, someone who has worked as a medical lab technician for ten years has learned a great deal about the technical characteristics of lab work, but many interactions over the years have shaped his view of people. He has learned how people react to the stress of a potentially serious illness, how they react when told good news about a loved one, how his peers react when they are stressed by an exceptionally long day of work, and on and on. Send him to a workshop on how to deal with terminal patients, and he will come to the class with real-life experiences that he will use to evaluate your lesson plan. Even if he is very interested in learning he will have his own ideas about the subject. You are not dealing with an empty slate; this learner has life experiences to draw upon.

Adult learners will challenge everything an instructor says, not to be recalcitrant, but rather because they have experiences that form the basis for their view of life and living. Every time a trainer provides an insight that goes against their life experience or the conclusions they have drawn from it, adult learners will want to challenge the trainer. If an adult has had significant experience, he can become stubborn about learning the concept or the data. When there is a direct contradiction between the lesson and his life experience, the learner is likely to choose the life experience.

This is a critical concept. Adult learners benefit from experience, but they may also be influenced by events that created a mistaken conclusion. A trainer of adults must distinguish between a valid conclusion that results from experience and a conclusion that is flawed. If it is valid, the adult learner may actually contribute important knowledge to the class. If it is flawed, the trainer must find a constructive way to help the associate "unlearn" the conclusion.

Further, no new idea will be accepted as meaningful if it cannot be put to a practical use. Tell a lab technician that people are afraid of the needles that are used to draw blood and you will see a big yawn. Tell the technician that the key to easing that anxiety can be learned from the tricks used by magicians and the learner may challenge the applicability or value of the idea but is likely to listen with interest. Tell the technician that magicians are able to create illusions because they can direct the audience to a distracting event, which allows them to perform the trick, and the technician may now understand the concept. He may recognize that a meaningful distraction, such as shaking the person's arm, could be the way to make a patient more relaxed for the insertion of the needle.

The message here is not that adult learners are stubborn. Quite the contrary. Some of the most dedicated learning anywhere happens in an adult classroom, where the learners are truly motivated to absorb knowledge and skills required to achieve their dreams. These aspirations help to stimulate even bigger leaps of growth, personal improvement, and development. Watching a motivated adult learner is a joy and watching your own associates learn and develop can be a thrill for even the most experienced leader.

Using practical applications of classroom learning is one of the great tools available to adult trainers. When in doubt, have adults do practical exercises and have them bring real-life problems from their own job. Get adult learners involved. Stay away from lectures and trainer-directed show and tell. Have adult learners do the show and tell. Many times a class can be the better teacher than the trainer. Why let the years of experience in the room go to waste? Harness the experience as a way of helping the group learn. This kind of training requires careful planning and good control, but done well, it is a fantastic way for adults to learn.

Although most work leaders are not formal trainers, the fact remains that a formal classroom-like setting can often be helpful in developing a work unit's staff. If you are training in a classroom setting with your own work unit, practical exercises are a great way to facilitate learning and at the same time get management tasks accomplished. As an example, assume that what you are trying to teach your staff is how to set goals for their work responsibilities. In the closest conference room, after you have taken time to describe the goal-setting process and explain why setting expectations is so critical to their success, break them into groups of two or four. Then separate the groups and have all the individuals do goal setting for their own job. Once they have completed their goals, then have each present the goals to the other group members for a critique. Without a doubt, the group's critiques are likely to be more stringent, yet more acceptable, than if you as work leader provided that feedback.

WORK LEADERS TIP   How to Interest an Adult Learner

Adult learners can be either the best students or the worst students. In some ways, it will be on your shoulders whether they achieve success.

Avoid the "Show and Tell" approach used by typical classroom teachers. Use the Conference method exclusively. This method provides for a combination of traditional telling by the instructor and participative dialogue with the students. It gives adults the opportunity to contribute the life experiences to the learning. All participants can also have practical exercises that reinforce the learning process.

Here are some additional ideas to turn the challenge of training adults into a great opportunity for learning and success.

- *Use lots of "practical exercises" that feel like real life.*

- *Use real-life, hands-on examples.*

- *Have students solve a real problem or answer a real inquiry.*

- *Do not have adult students sit for long.*

- *Be prepared to be challenged and to be wrong—and to admit to it.*

- *Be prepared to be challenged and to be right—gracefully.*

- *Do not act like a boss. Act like a teacher. Be patient. Not all ideas will sink in quickly.*

- *Theory is for graduate school. Teach them what they need to do the job.*

Coaching

Remember the old saying, "If the student failed to learn, the teacher failed to teach."

The teacher may have the responsibility to assure learning, but the learner must be committed to absorb and understand. The mentor must focus on creating an environment where the learner can find his own way. This is no place for orders. It is a place for coaching.

Coaching is the process of a mentor providing the help required to encourage discovery by a learner. A coach can try to tell a learner what to do, but the skepticism of adult learners inevitably thwarts such a process. If we seek to help people learn, we are really providing them with the energy for self-development. If you ever played a sport, you may have experienced the best of what coaching can be. Great coaches train the mind and the body to achieve more than the individual could have imagined. They inspire and they teach. They inspire with energy, enthusiasm, and love. They create an environment where athletes want to achieve. In addition, they teach the necessary skills and help athletes learn how to execute them with precision and excellence. Good coaches love, set expectations, assign talent to the right positions, develop abilities, evaluate performance, provide rewards, and are constantly growing their own competence through self-improvement.

As a work leader, you are asked to lead your staff, all day, every day. Developing the skills of your staff is a daily routine, not just done for a couple of hours at the end of the day.

81

Each time you work on a technical task with an associate, that time is an opportunity to coach your staff. Each time associates have a positive experience, it increases the probability that they will learn. Each time you pass up an opportunity to help them learn, you have lost ground in the effort to achieve excellence from your staff and to meet or exceed the organization's expectations of your work unit. To lead a peak performance organization you must commit more time to coaching your staff, helping them grow may be your highest priority as a leader. When they grow, your unit's performance will grow and peak performance will be the end result.

WORK LEADERS TIP — Teaching and Coaching, Are They the Same?

Teachers can coach and coaches can teach, but they are not doing the same jobs. Teachers tend to focus on knowledge; coaches tend to focus on skills. When we teach people what to do, we are giving them knowledge; when we coach them, we are helping them use the new knowledge.

Good coaching means

- *Showing how to do a task*
- *Asking why someone did a task*
- *Observing what was done and making suggestions for improvement*
- *Helping with a task when it is too complex*
- *Praising success*
- *Encouraging risk taking*
- *Providing constructive and corrective feedback*
- *Teaching facts and knowledge when required*

•*Supporting failure with solutions*

•*Answering questions when asked*

•*Offering help without threat of criticism*

Good coaching is not

•*Giving orders*

•*Giving punishment*

•*Demanding success*

•*Giving instructions and walking away*

•*Withholding support*

•*Using emotional pressure*

•*Being intolerant of mistakes*

With Love, Patience Can Coexist with Persistence

If you are a work leader, you probably got the job because you had high standards and expectations of yourself. Those same high standards and expectations probably also made you a leader quickly. Most organizations react very quickly when they find a high-potential, high-energy performer. When you became the leader, you expected, or at least wanted, your staff to go into high gear and follow your example. You probably found that they were moving much more slowly and less effectively toward your goals. Impatience set in.

Such is the plight of a strong individual performer promoted to leader. Patience is probably not your strong suit, yet excessive impatience will lead to frustration. If your expectations exceed their abilities or their current level of knowledge and skill development, staff members will get frustrated quickly. If this impatience is not addressed through careful development plans, your staff will conclude that there is no level of performance that will satisfy you and ultimately they will leave the organization looking for a more accepting and nurturing boss.

Small steps are a critical part of individual development. Small victories are the key to large change. Seldom does the process of human development reflect a dramatic shift from old ignorance to new enlightenment. Most of us learn incrementally and find that our knowledge gains results from adding together small bits of new knowledge. Such must be our approach to the development of raw talent. Each hour of each day should be designed to help your associates grow just one step at a time. Rome was not built in a day nor was your knowledge or that of the organization. It took you time to arrive at your current level; it will take time for your associates to develop as well.

The key to changing behavior—and that is in many ways what you are doing when you focus on developing an associate—is to never let up. Much of the change you are seeking will not occur if you fail to follow-up on the effort. Your first priority must be to take every opportunity to reinforce the behavior you seek and extinguish every behavior you choose to avoid. Your staff will not get the message 100 percent of the time; hence, you must repeat and repeat and repeat. Never assume that a learner has learned. Keep up the focus, the emphasis, and the reinforcement. It will pay off.

Most work leaders have experienced a new policy or procedure that affects the job of an associate who has been doing the same tasks the same way for several years. The change probably makes the work much simpler. Yet, the longtime associate, after being trained and instructed to change to the new procedure, simply cannot see its merit. Quickly, it becomes obvious that he is not implementing the changes, and the work leader begins to get negative feedback on the performance of the unit.

Obviously, patience is required, but patience is not enough. If all you were to do is be patient, you might wait forever for the change to be effectively implemented. If you order the associate to comply, you are likely to have passive resistance that can be devastating to achieving expectations while at the same time creating a serious morale problem with him. If you fail to implement the change in order to avoid the conflict, you will fail. What you really need is "patient persistence." Understand the associate's emotional and habitual reluctance to change, but tenaciously focus on making certain that the change occurs.

The key to patient persistence is to stay focused on the goal of implementation while maintaining a softer touch. Empathy for the associate cannot degenerate into sympathy, but you must recognize that his sense of loss of control is a serious problem and must be handled over time. By giving persistent reminders, with a sensitive and loving tone in your voice and body language, each and every time you have an interaction with that associate, you will ultimately convince that person that on one hand you understand his concerns and on the other you are not going to give in to his resistance to the change. In addition, frequently sitting down with the associate and going through the changed procedure yourself to learn precisely how it impacts the job will be invaluable. Then you are part of the process and you can show the benefits from direct knowledge. All but the most recalcitrant associate will get the message and begin the painful process of compliance.

Empowerment and the Ability to Fail

No amount of mentoring, tutoring, or classroom instruction can prepare an associate for the on-the-spot actions that occur every day. Forced to make an immediate decision, an associate can synthesize the bits and pieces of prior training into new knowledge that is practical and sustainable in the daily workplace.

Giving your associates the ability, indeed the authority, to make decisions on their own without consulting a rulebook, is a critical component of empowerment. Empowerment does not mean ignoring the rules. Empowerment means that your associate is authorized to act in a manner that is in the best interest of the organization. You are saying to your associates that you trust their judgment to consider the same factors and to make much the same decision you would make under similar circumstances. Empowerment is giving authority to act based on trust.

Empowerment is a very strong vehicle for learning and growth. It is often amazing how well your associates will do when they know that the decisions they make are going to be the final decisions. If you have hired the right people and you have taught them well, then they will rise to the occasion. Yes, they will make judgment errors, but more often than not the lesson and the values you have instilled will carry the day.

If you hold the associates back by not allowing them the opportunity to succeed or fail, they will never mature to their full potential. The thrill of being the decision maker helps all of us focus on making correct decisions. With solid development, coaching, and mentoring, associates can be ready for that exhilaration of success. On the other hand, associates not well coached can go all the way from astounding success to disastrous failure. Empowerment can only happen when development has been thorough.

Allowing your new associates the opportunity to make decisions involves risk. The failure of an individual can cause the failure of the unit. You will be required to assess when to allow the empowerment to continue and when to rein it in.

86

WORK LEADERS TIP — When Do You Empower your Associates to Fail?

Work Leaders cannot sacrifice the mission of the unit. How do you use failure to develop the associates who work for you? Use it when the unit's performance is not threatened.

- *Give a machinist a task, specify the requirements, let him set up the run, and check the results.*

- *Give an accountant an account to reconcile. Then have another associate check it.*

- *Have a salesperson handle a prospect all the way through the sales process when it is not a major sale.*

- *Have a new customer service representative handle all calls during an hour. Monitor all the calls and give feedback.*

- *Allow a newly trained lawyer to write an entire brief. Then provide an edit and critique.*

- *Allow a newly licensed and certified hairstylist to handle a customer. Then give a critique.*

- *Have an accounts-receivable clerk handle all the transactions for a day. Review the work the next day.*

- *Have a new teller handle all the transactions at a window. Check the balancing at the end of the day.*

Ongoing Development

Not all development should focus on job skills. Encouraging personal growth is not just good for an associate, it is good for the organization. The whole person comes to work each day and associates who know and understand themselves have more time to know and understand their work. Far too many staff members spend half their lives searching for themselves and the rest of the time just "getting by" at work. An associate cannot be productive if his day is consumed by self-doubt or worry over personal inadequacy. It is not the leader's responsibility to fund such efforts to find inner-confidence, but it is an opportunity to encourage them.

Deciding how to encourage these efforts for personal discovery can be a challenge. On one hand, we must avoid appearing to act like amateur psychologists; on the other, we actually need to do just that. As work leaders, we are not therapists helping people work through their personal identity and psychological-well-being issues. We are, however, in many ways diagnosticians. We must be able to recognize psychological challenges that are having a negative impact on associate's performance. How we use the diagnosis to facilitate resolution of the problems is a sensitive and difficult matter.

As a work leader you should get all the professional help you can to facilitate increased wellness in your staff. This is one of those times when consultation with your superior is probably the best advice. If your organization has a human resources department, then go there for help. If the problem

87

is important enough, it may be necessary to have an organizational process that refers the individual to a therapist or a social service agency or even to a private-sector support such as a minister or counselor. If you have a relationship with the associate or the associate discusses the problem with you, then you might be able to suggest that the associate seek help. It is imperative that you not damage your working relationship by appearing to interfere in the personal life of an associate; hence getting professional support in handling this type of situation is always the best course of action.

What responsibility do your staff members have for their own development? Have they created their own development plans? Have you asked them to write out those plans and then commit to their accomplishment? Have you reviewed and approved them? How do you decide what extraordinary training or development is required by your staff? Do you have those programs already established? If not, you should create a program that can be used as a general development tool for the entire unit, not just one or more staff members.

Your commitment to supporting continual development of associates should also extend to broadening knowledge beyond that required for the day-to-day tasks of the job. A course in art history may have very little to do with your work environment, but it can have everything to do with the development of a person who appreciates aesthetic beauty. In turn, it can influence an employee's ability to appreciate the value of the organization and its support of the arts in the community. The same could be said for a course in biology, which can help an individual appreciate the need to preserve the environment. In turn, it can help that same associate recognize, and even get involved in, the efforts of the organization to preserve the environment at the workplace. In short, seldom does a learning experience go to waste. Organizations should encourage general educational development. Those that can afford the expense should continue to subsidize advanced education as they are able, but they should also encourage learning in any formal or informal setting that helps associates grow.

Don't just *allow* your staff to self-improve, *encourage* it. Expanded knowledge helps your associates grow. On the job, you must allow them to learn tasks they do not need to know. One day, their knowledge may have a profound impact on your ability to fulfill the organization's needs. Today's seemingly extraneous knowledge may lead to tomorrow's promotion from within. Let the B clerk learn about the A clerk's job. Someday you may need another A clerk. The added cost of satisfying the intellectual curiosity of an associate is trivial in comparison to the cost of ignorance.

Just as importantly, if you believe that workplace improvements can and should come from the people in the workplace, then increased knowledge and skills will enhance associates' ability to contribute to employee-driven change through suggestion systems, quality control circles, and other employee participation systems. Harness the power of the staff members, instead of stifling them. Their growth can enhance the organization's growth.

Do you have a staff member who has received all of the training required by your organization but is still not performing to expected levels? What do you think you could do to facilitate a development experience that could make a real difference for your staff member? Why have you not done it? If you could do anything you wanted, how would you develop or train your staff member? Weak performers may well be the result of inadequate training and development. Your weak performers can be a clue to a failure of the development process, and that should be the first place you look for improvement. Create a list of the shortcomings of your weakest staff member and create a development plan that will provide the changes required to improve his performance. Compare that plan to the training and development plans already in place. If there is a disconnect, then talk to the training department about the problem.

Continuing growth is essential, even when excellence has been achieved. Keep the pressure on and push your associates to continuously improve. Complacency is a serious problem for a developing associate. The need for continuous improvement is never greater than when the staff members are fully comfortable with their current level of knowledge. As they lose the thrill of growth, they will become bored and may decide to leave to find something more exciting. Those who stay will settle into a comfortable rut, and inevitably their performance will deteriorate or worse, they will fail. Standing still is not possible. The choice is between moving forward and falling behind.

Focus on the Stars

Your toughest challenge may be to focus your efforts on your strongest associates, not the weakest. Anyone who loves people is likely to feel a strong desire to provide support to the problem members of an organization. It's tempting to play amateur psychologist or social worker and try to modify behavior. You could spend much of your daily routine working on all the underperforming staff, committed to making them a success. But when you place your focus on helping the weak, you leave the strong to fend for themselves.

I learned this lesson from a candidate for a senior management position in my organization. During the interview, I asked him to tell me about a time when he had taken a problem employee and helped that person to become an excellent associate. His answer shocked me. He said he had never been successful in transforming a truly weak employee and that he had never really spent much time trying. He had been given advice early on from his mentor that he should spend almost all of his development time (80 percent or more) with high-potential people and help them become great, leaving the weaker associates with only the remaining 20 percent of his time.

Since this idea violated everything I then believed about leadership, I did not hire the candidate. As fate would have it, my very next meeting that day was with a manager who had already taken up much of my time the day before because he had made a serious managerial mistake. I spent an hour with him explaining why his decision was simply wrong and destructive to the organization, but he could not understand why I was making such a fuss over the issue.

Right after that meeting, my best manager came to me with a problem he needed help with. At this point, I only had five minutes before I had to meet with my boss. By the time he laid out the problem, it was time for me to leave. As I was going out the door, he said to me in a rather frustrated tone, "Gerry, I really needed help and you couldn't give me five minutes. I guess I will have to find somebody else to help me."

I knew I had let him down. He was my best manager and deserved better. That night I was forced to look at myself in a very painful way. That candidate was right. I began to change my thinking about leadership development. This lesson must be remembered if you are going to build an organization committed to Peak Performance.

You are not going to achieve peak performance with mediocrity. Your company may be better than another company, or your unit may be better than another unit, but you will not achieve peak performance until you have stars dominating the staff and you are spending the time developing the stars. The key to this concept is the core principle that a star is not always the star performer. A star is that person who has the potential of being the outstanding associate yet may not have arrived at that level of achievement. A star is defined by long-term potential, not by current performance.

Focusing your development efforts on your stars is not an elitist philosophy; it is simply the best use of your time. When you help a star develop to become a star performer, you have not only served yourself well, but also you have served the individual and the organization as a whole. Ten minutes of helping a star to do a better job will pay greater dividends than ten hours with an unsatisfactory performer. You should not write off the unsatisfactory performer, but you must make certain that the star gets the benefit of your leadership first. The investment will have a phenomenal return.

Ask yourself which staff member is your potential star? Has that person been adequately trained by you? Is that person performing at his capability? What can you do that would make the person your company's highest performer? Armed with the answers to these questions, sit down with that person and tell him you want to develop a plan for advancing his growth. Give that associate the opportunity to participate in the development of the plan. You will get his attention and you may even get him energized by your commitment.

Share Your Knowledge:
The More *They* Know, the More *You* Grow

In order to be a great teacher, a leader must first know how to share. Sharing means being willing to give up exclusive knowledge to associates. For many leaders, knowledge is power, and by not sharing with their associates, they protect their own position and assure continued job security.

However, as a Work Leader you are the key to the organization's ability to replicate itself. You hold the detailed knowledge about the organization. Your work unit is, by our definition, where the works gets out. It is where the parts are made, the assembly is completed, the research is accomplished, and where the breakthrough in new products occurs. Someday you may move on, but if your unit does not have a leader, it will fail in the core mission of the enterprise.

Indeed, the inevitable result of successful development is that the mentee will no longer need the mentor. Do your job well and you will not be needed. Your entire concept of leadership must include the willingness—indeed the commitment—to train your associates to eventually become leaders. This transfer of leadership is essential for the survival of an organization.

Your ability to transfer knowledge to your associates is the true measure of your ability to lead. When they have learned and can function without you, you have liberated them and yourself. You will be freed to focus on your own success; however, if you continue to guard your knowledge jealously, you will thwart your own development. This is because only when your organization can succeed without you, can you expect to move on to your next assignment.

If you do your job well, you will be growing leaders, not followers. This means that as you develop your associates, you are developing your organization's future management. Many leaders fail to develop staff to replace them. The two tragedies of that are (1) we never have anybody to replace us as we look toward our next promotion; (2) they never have the staff to grow their existing responsibilities. A leader who is threatened by followers who become leaders is not a leader for the future. Always be prepared to groom not only your successor, but also your boss's successor. Try hiring and developing people who are better than you think you are. What happens is remarkable. They will bloom and you will get even better. That is a win-win-win situation. They win, you win, and the organization wins!

WORK LEADERS TIP — Look for Holes in Their Knowledge and Fill Them

It is imperative that you teach every associate in your unit how to do his job and do it well. The organization relies on that knowledge. Pass on what you know by making it easy for your staff to learn.

- *Do not discourage questions by making fun of ignorance. You were ignorant once.*

- *If your associates know what you do, then you will have time for other tasks your boss needs done.*

- *Make it fun for your staff to learn. Reward their learning.*

- *Most associates want to learn more. Give them new challenges every day.*

- *Knowledge is power. When your staff knows, they have power and that increases yours.*

- *You will never get promoted if you are the sole source of knowledge.*

93

CASE STUDY

Stan had been a trainer for leadership development for nearly two years and he was under a lot of pressure. Now the vice president was coming. His last visit had been a disaster. The VP had asked Stan how the program had changed since he started teaching it, and Stan was taken back with the question.

"I have not changed it at all," he said, "I was told that the program was developed by an expensive outside consultant five years ago and that top management did not want it changed."

At that point Stan had had a very uncomfortable feeling that he was in trouble, and he did not really understand why.

Karen, his boss, had given him a look that made him feel worthless and then said, "I did not think that Stan should tamper with the successful program, and besides, he does not have the program development experience that it would take to modify the program. I think that I am the only one in the section that has the knowledge, and I simply have not had the time to teach him. Besides, that really is my job and not his."

At that point the VP said to Stan, "I am disappointed that you have not taken the initiative to modify and update the program. I thought that you had a bachelor's degree in adult education and *a master's in executive leadership. That seems to me to be more than enough background, Karen. You should work with Stan so that we can better utilize his educational background."*

That little incident had created quite a problem for Stan, and the situation had been getting worse. Ever since that meeting three months ago, Stan had tried to get Karen to work with him to show him what he needed to do to make program modifications.

Always Karen's answer was the same: "Stan, I do not have the time, and when I do, I will do the changes myself. Just concentrate on being a good trainer; I will worry about program development."

Lately, Karen had become more upset than ever and less willing to help Stan grow. All of the program development reference materials were in Karen's office, and it was clear that she was not going to share her knowledge. Now the VP was coming back, and Stan knew that he would be asking the same questions. Unfortunately, Stan would have the same unacceptable answers. If he told the truth, Karen would be even more upset, and if he did not, then the VP would think that Stan was lazy and unwilling to improve himself. What a dilemma. The day before the visit, Stan got a very bad cold and was forced to stay home. Three days later, he quit.

Questions

1. Why did Stan quit?

2. Why did Karen not work with Stan? Would Karen have been able to improve Stan's performance?

3. What could Stan have done to fix the situation so that he would get what he needed to develop his skills?

4. Do you believe that Karen has a responsibility to further her own improvement? What should her boss be doing to help her?

Evaluation
Leaders Succeed By Making Judgements

A quick review: We started with *Love* for our associates, established *Expectations*, made the right *Assignment* and then worked at *Development* of our associates. Most readers would probably guess that *Evaluation* of performance is the logical next step. Yet if it is so obvious, why is evaluation so often ignored, postponed, or forgotten? How many times in your career have you waited a whole year for your annual performance appraisal only to find out that you have not been doing the job?

Evaluation Is Hard Work; With Love It Might Be Less Stressful

We have returned to the principle of love many times however. Nowhere is this concept more important than in evaluation, which is often the most personally challenging and potentially painful aspect of being a Work Leader. Nothing you do can be more helpful or damaging to your associates. Do evaluations well and they can be exhilarating for you and your team. Do them badly and they can be devastating for both. No wonder this step in the Work Leaders Seven Principles is so frequently avoided.

For many Leaders, performing evaluations is one of their least enjoyable tasks. Why do so many dislike it? You may say you only have a problem giving evaluations when people are not doing the job. If that is true, then assuming that only 10 percent or so of associates are failures, does that mean 90 percent of the time you like doing them? In fact, giving performance reviews to outstanding performers can be just as hard as giving performance reviews to unsatisfactory performers. The truth is they are very hard work.

Ironically, we ourselves want to receive meaningful and timely performance reviews. This is especially true if we think we have done a great job. You would think that if it is personally desirable for us to get feedback, then we should want to do the same for our associates. Yet the evidence is clear; most leaders would rather work three shifts in a row than have a single negative feedback session with a subordinate.

Five Reasons Why Leaders Avoid Evaluations

For Leaders, evaluation is work that they know must be done but which they tend to avoid at almost all costs. Leaders find these evaluations tough for several reasons:

1. Most of us simply do not enjoy being judgmental about others, especially people we work with every day. We would like to avoid such conversations because they create tension.

2. We don't want to cope with disagreement from the recipient of the evaluation. Associates are likely to agree with positive feedback, and they are just as likely to disagree with negative feedback. Most bosses would avoid the conflict if they could, and many do by simply ignoring the evaluation process. The stress is intensified if the performance review is tied to pay, as most often it is. Even an outstanding performer, in a meaningful and honest evaluation, will almost always require some negative feedback. But since we generally do not want to complicate or alienate a positive performance, we

often give a performance review that is all positives, with no negatives. Consequently, we never address the issues that call for action.

3. In order to evaluate, we need criteria. That means that we need to have expectations that we can compare to the job performance. If we have not made the expectations list specific and measurable, we have a very difficult time measuring against the benchmark. The worse we are at setting expectations, the more we will worry and procrastinate when it comes time for evaluations. Ultimately, the result will be an evaluation that is weak to inadequate. And compound the tension that already exists whenever negative feedback is given.

4. The documentation required for an evaluation takes a lot of time that we would much rather spend getting the work out. Often we are required to complete forms that make us record factors that we are not really tracking or that we think are irrelevant. Worse still, we sometimes wish we had focused on those items, but now it is too late, and we are going to have to fake the results.

5. We usually are convinced that the people who are doing a good job know we think they are great and that evaluations for them are a waste of time. We want to tell them everything is fine and not much more. We give them no evaluation, just a quick comment and a salary increase. Now everybody is happy and we can go back to work.

The simple fact is that all of these reasons reflect a failure to assure performance. Ken Blanchard says it all: "Everyone has peak performance potential. You just need to know where they are coming from and meet them there."[26] The problem is you can never meet them there if you never tell them where you are. How can you develop your associates if you never give them insight into their current level of performance?

WORK LEADERS TIP

Ask Yourself These Questions and See Why Appraisals Are tough

- *Have you ever been surprised by a remark on your annual performance appraisal? Why? What did you do about it?*

- *When was the last time you got feedback from your boss? Was it positive feedback? Was it negative? What did you do about the feedback? Did your boss discuss how you could improve?*

- *Think of your worst staff member. When was the last time you gave that person a formal performance appraisal? When was the last time you actually sat down and discussed performance since that time? What happened?*

- *Think of your best staff member. When was the last time you gave that person any feedback at all? What was it about? What was the outcome?*

- *What happened when you had your last performance appraisal with a staff member. What was the result of that meeting? Has there been any change in performance from that person?*

If This Were Simple,
Then Everybody Would Be a Leader

Giving a performance review to an outstanding performer can really make you feel good. For most of us, praise is a great deal more fun that criticism. It is only when we are forced to give strong, highly critical, and negative feedback that most of us wish we could ask somebody else to do it for us.

One senior executive routinely did just that. He would give all of the positive reviews himself and leave the negative reviews and even firings to his director of human resources. This man was incapable of facing his responsibilities as a leader. He always wanted to feel good and could not face the difficult task of confronting another human being with the honest and caring truth. Worse still, he convinced many people in the organization that he was such a warm and caring person that he could not bring himself to hurt anybody. What a fraud. If he truly cared for (loved) his associates, he would have recognized that it was his duty to do everything he could to help them succeed even if on occasion that meant telling them something they did not want to hear.

Loving humans requires helping them, even if the truth is painful. People with no understanding of their weaknesses are living in a fantasy world. It is our duty to help our associates deal with their own shortcomings as well as to help them understand their strengths. Just as in a manufacturing environment, we can only improve the process by understanding its weaknesses. Improvement cannot happen if we do not know what needs to be improved, and without improvement there can be no excellence.

You will hear this again, but remember that you are not trying to create capability; you are working to enhance it. Do not waste your time on the hopeless, but where there is hope, give it a real commitment. In their book, *First, Break All the Rules*, Buckingham and Coffman say it simply, "People don't change that much. Don't waste time trying to put in what was left out. Try to draw out what was left in. That is hard enough."[27]

WORK LEADERS TIP

Get Yourself Ready for
That Tough Feedback Session

As you prepare yourself for a feedback session? Here are some thoughts that might help you keep your resolve:

- *Remind yourself that you are a great Leader, and great Leaders evaluate performance.*

- *Remember, it is part of the job.*

- *Remember, procrastinating only puts off the inevitable.*

- *Associate performance must be better or our unit is at risk.*

- *How can he improve if I do not tell him about the problem?*

- *She deserves honest feedback for her outstanding performance.*

- *My associates deserve better performance from him.*

- *Her behavior is abusive and unacceptable. Tough love may be the only solution.*

- *This associate is not right for the job. She is probably miserable as well.*

- *This associate has broken the value of integrity and trust. He should have been terminated yesterday.*

- *This associate has alienated our customers many times. They pay the bills.*

- *His performance is negatively impacting the others in the unit.*

- *I have worked with her for six months, but she has done nothing to improve. Enough is enough.*

- *I have spent too much time trying to help a hopeless case. Others need my time.*

Even Daily May Be Too Seldom

Compounding the problem of giving effective evaluations is that all too often they are relegated to a once-a-year activity. Nothing could be worse. The practice of waiting a full year to give direct, formal evaluation and performance feedback is unfair to the associate and illogical for the organization's interests. Evaluation must be an activity that is tied to the daily performance of the individual, not to the convenience of a process. We cannot expect associates to know what we do not tell them. Either positive or negative messages about behavior or performance must be communicated at the time of the event, not a month or a year later. How can we expect change if we make no attempt to inform associates about their performance?

Annual reviews do not work to the benefit of the associate or the organization. Over forty years ago, Douglas McGregor, in his classic book *The Human Side of Enterprise*, wrote about the annual performance appraisal and his message is still on the mark:

103

> The semiannual or annual appraisal is not a particularly efficient stimulus to learning for another reason: It provides "feedback" about behavior at a time remote from the behavior itself. People do learn and change as a result of feedback. In fact, it is the only way they learn. However, the most effective feedback occurs immediately after the behavior. The subordinate can learn a great deal from a mistake, or a particular failure in a performance, provided it is analyzed while all the evidence is immediately at hand. Three or four months later, the likelihood of effective learning from that experience is small. It will be still smaller if the superior's generalized criticism relates to several incidents spread over a period of months.[28]

A behavioral psychologist, such as B.F. Skinner, would say that if you fail to reinforce desired behavior, it will eventually disappear. And if you fail to punish undesirable behavior, you will encourage it to continue. Classical Freudian psychology would hold that behavior will persist until an individual understands the core reasons for its existence. In any case, allowing an associate to go without an honest evaluation of behaviors and performances is a classic sign that leaders have failed the love test.

If we really loved our associates, we would not allow them to drift with no idea as to how they stand. Unfortunately, too many of us fail our associates and give them, at best, severely delayed feedback.

WORK LEADERS TIP Give One-Minute Feedback—Immediately

Whenever it is obvious that an associate's behavior was either exceptionally good or obviously inappropriate is the right time for one minute feedback.

Here are some good rules for a one-minute feedback session:

- *Do it immediately.*

- *Waste no time.*

- *Make your comments clear and crisp.*

- *Be calm and yet firm.*

- *Refer directly to what just happened.*

- *If it is positive feedback, be positive, warm, and friendly.*

- *If it is negative feedback, make it firm but gentle.*

- *Above all, make the session short and focused only on the event, not a history lesson on other events.*

Make Certain You Really Have the Associate's Attention

One of the great problems in giving feedback is making certain it is received. Most of us have a difficult time receiving feedback, and when we do, we only listen to what we either believe or want to believe. Further, we all have a tendency to believe only comments that are positive. Think about the last time you were asked to list your strengths and weaknesses. In all likelihood, you did a good job on the strengths and not so well on the weaknesses. The weaknesses you listed were probably qualities you actually considered strengths. Most of us have a difficult time admitting to real weaknesses, and if we do, we generally find a way to excuse them. We tend to do the same with evaluations.

Think about the last time you asked an associate the question, "Tell me about your weaknesses." The associate probably answered with comments like (1) "I am impatient when my staff falls short of its goals" or (2) "I set standards that some people think are too high" or (3) "I work too many hours in a day." In all likelihood, the associate really believed that these observations could be viewed by some as weaknesses but only if the behavior was extreme. In most cases, impatience is good when it looks for excellence, high standards are great when they challenge associates to achieve excellence, hard work is a positive when it reflects an associate's commitment to achievement. In short, the comments really reflect pride, not weakness.

In addition, most people have a tendency to block out bad news because they find it much more enjoyable to go through life hearing only good news. Worse still, because people often do not want to face negatives, they hear them, but do not process them. Thus, a counseling session by a concerned boss can often be totally lost because the comments are heard but not listened to. The sound hits the eardrum but does not make its way to the conscious mind for processing. How many times have you shut out a speaker's words by simply turning off your attention? Your associates will do the same to you.

You are likely to have had a number of associates who received frequent feedback yet later tell you that they have

105

never been told about their failings. You probably have been frequently frustrated and bewildered by these denials. Try this technique. Tell the associate that she should listen carefully because you are turning on the counseling switch, at which time you walk over to the light switch on the wall and turn on the bright ceiling lights. This bit of drama often works. By the time you sit down at the table, your associate will be clearly focused on what you have to say. Although a playful approach may not work with all associates, you need to do whatever it takes to get their attention. The "counseling switch" idea works much of the time, but not always. Some associates either do not get the idea or are offended by the gamesmanship. Remember that you are leading a team but that each member of that team is an individual. Some ideas work with some and not with others. Keep trying. For most people, there is something that will get their attention, but it may not always be obvious. Always use the name of the person, and always make the feedback session private, not in front of other associates. Whatever you do, make certain that the associate understands that you are serious and expect her attention. When you give feedback, particularly negative feedback, literally announce that you are about to begin a counseling session. This suggests that what is about to occur involves the associate's performance and must be remembered.

WORK LEADERS TIP — How To Get and Keep Their Attention—Other Ideas

Try some of these statements when you need to get an associate's attention.

- *To be direct: "Frank, I want you to know this is a formal feedback session."*

- *For the receptive type: "Joe, I have some thoughts that might help you improve."*

- *For the chronic failure: "Barb, we have talked about this problem before."*

- *For the serious event: "John, you just made a serious mistake; let's talk."*
- *For the worrier: "Sally, you have asked me to give you feedback."*
- *For the rude one: "Kim, I would like to discuss your outburst."*
- *For a victory: "Stephen, you just did a great job, thank you."*
- *For an obvious error: "Mark, I am very concerned about they way you handled that."*

Talk about Behavior First

We all know that job performance is what we must be focused on. Our expectations are the driving force for our leadership position. If your associate's performance is either superior or unsatisfactory, we must provide feedback to them. However, we must also understand that all individual performance is a function of behavior. If associates come to the job with severe behavioral limitations, then their job performance will be negative. If they come to the job with certain essential weaknesses that, if improved, could substantially improve job performance, then we have a duty to provide feedback if we truly love them and care about their success.

If what people are and how they behave can make a difference in expectations, then we must as leaders focus on those. Qualities like intelligence, the ability to reason, to think logically, to articulate ideas and to function under stress as well as the capacity to relate to people, the intensity of the work ethic, and much more all help to define what people are and how they will perform. You need to know your associates. It is not enough to say, "You did a great job." You need to understand them as whole beings.

A good way to do this is to use "trait reviews." These are not report cards on behavior like children used to get in elementary school, but they have one critical resemblance: they give feedback on characteristics of behavior that can

107

have influence an associate's ability to perform. The goal must be to focus on results, on performance compared to expectations; however, it is equally important to give feedback on those traits that either help or hinder success. If an associate has difficulty developing working relationships with her peers, that weakness is going to have a major influence on her ability to achieve results in almost any organization. Effective feedback, counseling, and developmental support are critical if the associate is going to become a superior performer. If you choose to avoid this sensitive psychological issue, you will cheat the employee of support that could make a huge difference in not just current but future assignments. If you really have the capacity to love an associate, you must take on this topic and attempt to help the individual deal with the shortcoming. Of course, how effective you are will depend in large measure on the receptivity of the individual; however, your performance is critical also. If you give feedback being sensitive to the mindset of the recipients, in other words, if you "walk in their shoes," you will have a much better chance to be heard and heeded than if you chose to preach and moralize.

Making speeches may make you feel better, but the tone may also make an associate reject what you have to say. The associate must acknowledge the weakness and accept it as an issue that requires change. No amount of preaching will have any value at all if you alienate the associate. Only when the problem is acknowledged by the individual can a solution be found and implemented. By the same token, if you never raise the issue because you think that psychology is not your role, then you will probably fail to provide your contribution to the development of a superior performer. This part of evaluation is hard work, but it is what leaders must do if they are to play their role well. Helping to make winners is not always easy, but it will always be rewarding for a leader who begins with love.

Trait Reviews Are Tough, But They Are Great

A great deal can be gained from taking the time to talk to your associates about how their traits and behaviors affect their job performance. The good news is that most of the issues you are talking about influence job performance; the bad news is that you may misjudge the situation and then have to argue with the associate. In addition, you are going to be doing something that is not normally comfortable: tell people how you perceive them. You will be focusing on insights that you have drawn from working with them. You will be talking about them, and their behavior, not just their job performance. We think about people's behavior all the time, but seldom do we tell them what we think. Yet results at work are almost always tied to behaviors. You may not be able to change associates' behavior, but if they know what you have observed, they may conclude that they must attempt to deal with these issues.

Incidentally, in the event that you give some feedback and are challenged, a simple way to deal with an objection is to acknowledge that you know you may be wrong, but that is why you are talking about it. You are trying to get a better understanding of her, so that you, and she, can judge her ability to improve. Tell her that you will spend some more time thinking about it. This acknowledges that you could be wrong without saying definitively that you are. Being right is not the issue. Giving the associate this information makes it possible for her to understand the perceptions that exist.

The content of a "trait review" follows a simple structure, but it must always be part of a comprehensive review of the associate's performance. Never do a trait review without tying it to a performance evaluation. The goal is to give associates an opportunity to see that their performance can be tied to their personal traits. Also never tell associates that you are evaluating them on their personal traits. Performance evaluations should be based on the associate's achievement of results. But the trait review gives the associate an opportunity to correct issues that affect performance.

The Process Is Critical

Always begin a trait review with an introduction explaining to the associate that you are not a psychologist, but rather a leader who has great interest in understanding her so that you help her grow and improve. Then give a general review of the categories you will discuss and the reasons for discussing them.

I.   The Mind

Mental skills certainly affect job performance because most jobs today can be viewed as "knowledge worker" positions. How the individual uses those mental skills is critical to the ability to learn as well as execute job functions. In this part of the trait review, you will give the associate feedback on abilities such as:

a.   The ability to achieve effective reasoning

b.   Problem solving skills

c.   Systematic and logical thinking

d.   The ability to employ analytical skills to create new approaches

e.   The speed with which the associate learns new ideas

II.   The Emotions

Emotional stability and control is a critical requirement in any job environment because the individual must be reliable over an extended period of time and in a variety of situations. In this part of the trait review, you will give the associate feedback on characteristics such as:

a.   The ability to maintain emotional control

b.   Ability to deal with constructive feedback on work performance

c.   The associate's commitment to work

d.   The associate's self-confidence

e.   The ability to deal with change and stressful situations

f.   Ability to avoid personal problems from affect on-the-job performance

III.   The Knowledge

Every associate must be able to demonstrate a core knowledge and understanding of the work they are doing. In this part of the trait review, you will give the associate feedback on how you evaluate their job knowledge such as:

    a.   Understanding of business principles in general

    b.   Understanding of the specific work unit activities

    c.   Knowledge and understand of the organization as a whole

    d.   Knowledge of the specific job the associate is assigned to accomplish

    e.   The application of knowledge that contributes to required skills for the job

IV.   The Relationships

Any person in the workplace must ultimately deal with co-workers in order to be effective. In this part of the trait review, you will give the associate feedback on abilities such as:

    a.   The ability to work with colleagues

    b.   Capacity to develop a sound working relationship with you, the boss

    c.   Commitment to working as a team member

    d.   Capacity as a leader

    e.   Commitment and capability of the associate to develop cross-organizational relationships

    f.   Capacity to effectively handle customers, vendors, or any other professional relationships that impact the ability to achieve success on the job

V.   The Future

Any associate who is to be a star in an organization will need to be able to think about the long run. In this part of the trait review, you will give the associate feedback on abilities such as:

a. Seeing and understanding business growth opportunities

b. Willingness to develop plans for improvement in the organization

c. Commitment to establish plans for personal development

When you take the time to discuss these key characteristics, you demonstrate to an associate that you are committed to feedback. By sharing these thoughts, you give associates an opportunity to understand how you perceive them and how you believe they are perceived by the organization.

Love Means Honesty and Candor—Not Brutality

Giving effective feedback is hard work, but taking it is, too. Hearing negative words about our behavior or performance is painful for any individual. Consequently, when we are in a position to give feedback, we usually attempt to couch the words in the most appealing fashion we can.

If you have been exposed to any formal sales training, you were probably taught that you should always deal with negatives in a sales situation by attempting to focus on the positives instead. You were also probably told that you must make yourself communicate in a positive fashion in order to get an order from a resistant buyer. In this case, there is no doubt that the recipient of constructive feedback in an evaluation session will be a "reluctant buyer." Such training gives you all the more reason to walk carefully through the minefield of feedback.

However, providing candid and direct insight is better than trying to mask the truth and spare people the pain of confronting their weaknesses. Don't give associates an excuse to argue that they did not hear what you said. However, in spite of the need to be forthright, there is no reason to be brutal. Statements like, "That was stupid" are cruel and confrontational and will illicit a strong reaction. Saying, "You have failed" may be truthful, but it may also be so devastating that the associate may simply not listen. Try statements like "I think you have some areas that could be improved." This approach shows that you believe the associate can fix the problem and that the short-term failure can be overcome. It provides hope that the feedback will constructively improve the performance. Your goal should be to clearly and directly communicate the constructive evaluation, but you must continue to take all actions based on your ability to love.

Andy Grove in *High Output Management*, gives sound advice about delivering the assessment. "There are three *L's* to keep in mind when delivering a review: Level, Listen, and Leave yourself out."[29] By "level" he means to be honest, by "listen" he means just that. "Leave yourself out" means try to avoid the bias of your own thinking.

People Believe What They See: Write Objectively

Another way to deal with your associates' natural tendency to rationalize that they are doing an adequate job is to use the written word. The written word is a strong dose of reality. Seldom does anybody fail to get the message from written documentation. That is true for positive evaluations as well as negative ones. This impact, however, is not the only advantage. What you write out is much more likely to communicate the essence of your message because writing helps you to sort through the key concepts you want to communicate. In addition, you are much more likely to be careful about what you say if we put it into the written form. As further benefit, writing may help you to clarify your ideas or perhaps to even change them.

Many of us do not enjoy writing and may be convinced that writing evaluations is a waste of time. Typically, organizations require a written performance appraisal. The document we are discussing may satisfy the organization's expectations, but it is not for the organization, it is for you. It is your guide to helping your associate improve. You will be a better leader if you have the ability to give better evaluations.

Don't Accept the Blame

Giving an associate constructive feedback is only half the responsibility. The process of evaluation has one more critical step. You must also commit yourself to influencing their behavior. Of course, you cannot make the changes in behavior and performance; only the associate can do that. Your communications to associates must place the responsibility for the behavior and the performance squarely on their shoulders.

All too often, your associates will look to you to either explain their difficulties or to solve their challenges. At times you may be the cause of the difficulty, but in the vast majority of cases, this retort is simply an expression of frustration. The associate knows the problem exists, and puts the problem right back on you. Obviously you must consider carefully any assertion that the problem is your fault, but in most instances, you must not accept the burden. Individuals are, in the final analysis, responsible for their own behavior.

Get Plans to Fix the Problems and Follow Up Consistently

Evaluation is useless if there is no change in behavior or performance, and change takes conscious commitment, effort, and a deliberate plan of action. Planning is not just saying, "I plan to do a better job" or "I plan to be a better person." Planning is deciding what the goals are and how to know if they have been achieved. It takes defining specific actions required to make changes, laying out a timetable for doing them, establishing checkpoints along the way, and creating a mechanism to assess if the actions and results are really on track to accomplish the goals. All of that is hard work, and it requires a real commitment. An associate who has a sincere desire and commitment to improve will continue with the ongoing discipline required to achieve the steps on the journey to success. Without that commitment, most associates will fall well short of their original goals, and you will be having the same evaluation discussion later.

That is where a leader can come in. You must follow up on any evaluation. You cannot make the changes, you cannot enforce the commitment, but you can support it. A leader can take several actions to make certain that an associate has a reasonable chance for achieving success.

First, you can offer to help the individual develop a plan. Helping an associate work to set goals is a logical extension of your responsibility to establish expectations. By being involved in this process, you are clarifying and enhancing your role as leader. Further, if an associate has not been able to establish a format for the plan, you can help create a structure that works. After it is completed, offer to provide feedback on the plan.

One of the many values of being a part of the self-improvement-plan process is that it gives a leader the opportunity to validate the effectiveness of the evaluation feedback. If the plan truly addresses the issues raised in the evaluation, then, at a minimum, you can say that you have succeeded in communicating the need for improvement. If the plan does not, then you have an opportunity to refine the process before the associate wastes weeks or months of effort focusing on the wrong issues. This is hard work and requires a leader who feels the sense of love and commitment to the improvement of all associates as they search for their potential achievement level and fulfillment.

115

Second, you can ask associates how they are doing on their personal improvement plan. Simple though that question may be, it can have a profound effect. When the leader asks a question, the staff listens. When the leader listens to the answer and responds appropriately, the staff has been affected. Leaders should never underestimate the influence they have. You are the single most important person in the daily life of the associate. Your interest in them, your questions to them, are powerful.

Third, you can influence an associate by acknowledging improvement. You will look more closely in the next chapter at the power of this act, but suffice to say, when you recognize improvement, you have reinforced the behavior.

WORK LEADERS TIP

Before You Evaluate, Prepare

- Chose the one person in your unit that needs a counseling session most and prepare an outline of the discussion you will have with that person.

- Describe what you plan to do to deal with the most unsatisfactory performer in your unit. Create an action plan for dealing with that person. Be specific about what your expectation is for the result of your plan.

- Practice the session. Role play with yourself; build your confidence.

- Just to be prepared, assume that the session above was not successful. Now prepare a brief on a final session where you will terminate that person.

CASE STUDY

Fred was on his way to put in another boring day at work. He had been at the company for about ten years and in his current job for exactly twelve months. That may be why I have a meeting today with my supervisor, he thought. I am probably due for a salary increase, and she wants to tell me what it is.

Fred had had a tough adjustment to his last promotion. He kept the problems to himself, but he really did not like being a supervisor. He liked the people, but he *just did not like giving orders. His boss, Sally, had been there for a long time and all of the people on the staff were very much afraid of her. He had tried to become friendly with the staff, but Sally told him during his first week on the job that she would not tolerate "fraternization." He did not say anything to Sally, but he thought that idea was silly, and he did take coffee breaks with his staff quite a often. After many months, he had gotten to know the staff members well and liked them very much. The only problem he had was that many of them were not doing what Sally expected them to do. He just could not get them to perform. Fred thought, That may be what Sally wants to talk about today. I hope so, because I would like her advice on what to do. We really don't talk very often.*

When Fred walked over to Sally's office to start the meeting, Sally asked him in and told him to close the door. I have never seen her ask anybody to close the door, he thought, I wonder what is up?

"Fred," Sally began, "You have been here a year, and I need to give you your performance review. I do not know any easy way to say it, but it is just not working out. I have given you a full year to get the section in line, and it has not happened. Contrary to my instructions, you have fraternized with the staff, and your performance shows why it is a bad idea. You have missed all of your goals, and your staff is working at the worst productivity level in the entire department. Your evaluation comes up an unsatisfactory, and I am going to have to let you go."

Sally paused, and Fred thought his heart was going to come out of his chest. "I had no idea you were unhappy with my performance," he said. "What can I do to make it up?"

"Nothing. I have talked to Personnel and they are waiting for you to out-process. Please give me your keys to the files and take your personal belongings out of the desk and report to Personnel quickly. I wish you the best."

Questions/Discussion Points

1. How would you evaluate this performance appraisal? What was right? What was wrong with it?

2. Fred was surprised by the results of his conversation with his boss. How could Fred have been surprised? Was he not listening? Was he simply not very smart?

3. Was Fred's boss wrong? If you think so, what did Sally do wrong? How would you counsel her on her leadership?

4. Do you think that Fred has a cause for legal action against Sally and the company?

CHAPTER SIX

Rewards
An Organization Elicits the Behavior It Rewards

At a very early stage in my managerial career, I walked into the office of a new boss and saw a sign on his wall that read, "An organization elicits the behavior it rewards." This man ultimately became my most important mentor and his message on that sign has stayed with me ever since.

To use a simple analogy, a dog behind an invisible fence learns not to go outside the boundary because he gets an electric shock when he crosses it. By the same token, he learns to sit on command when he is given a treat for doing it correctly. In short, there are two ways to learn—one through threat or punishment, one through reward. Although we humans are far more complex than dogs, the same principles of learning can apply to us. The message in this chapter is be positive. Although punishment has some value, the value of rewards is far greater. We learn what we should be doing by being rewarded for the behavior.

As children we learn the word no or not very early. As we explore the new things we encounter, our parents often try to protect us from mistakes by telling us no. Work Leaders need to break the "Cycle of No." Every time you think of the word no as an answer or as a statement, try a positive version of that response. Focus on what *to* do, instead of what *not* to do.

WORK LEADERS TIP

Try the Positive First

- **Instead of** *"No, you may not have the day off."*

  Try *"I would like you to take next Thursday off, will that work for you?"*

- **Instead of** *"Do not leave that box in the middle of the room."*

  Try *"Please put the box in the corner; it will be safer for all of us."*

- **Instead of** *"I am very unhappy with the quality of your assembly work. You are going to have to stay tonight for another two hours to fix the re-work problems."*

  Try *"Yesterday you had great quality on your production. I would like to compliment you on that and ask you to help me learn why today's was so much less. Maybe we can find the problem and that way you will not be forced to stay overtime to rework all the problem pieces tomorrow."*

- **Instead of** *"You have been behaving very rudely toward your associates for several months. It must stop. If it does not, you are going to be either transferred or terminated."*

  Try *"Joe, I was very pleased just then when you spoke nicely to Frank. That is the way I would like you to treat everybody. If you do that, I think that your relationships with the other associates will improve and you will have a chance to be considered for promotion a great deal sooner."*

•*Instead of* "Sally, stop doing that it's the wrong way."

Try "Sally, here is what I would like you to do. This is going to save you a significant amount of time and energy."

Negative Feedback Creates Fear; Fear Creates Flight

Using rewards to reinforce desired behavior is better than using punishment to eliminate unacceptable behavior. The reason is simple: punishment can lead to serious negative reactions resulting from a fear of failure. Give adults the opportunity to be given an award for outstanding performance and they will focus on doing what it takes to achieve the goal. Tell adults that they will be fired if they fail to meet a goal and in all likelihood their focus will be on avoiding failure rather than striving for success. Fear can motivate, but it can also paralyze. If we fear something enough, we will spend our time attempting to avoid it. Achieving a goal because of fear will not assure a continued commitment to success. An associate may respond to a negative feedback session with an immediate surge of adrenaline-driven energy, but he may also feel long-term anger that can destroy effective learning and ultimately lead to resentment and resignation.

The emotion of fear at first causes a normal reaction of flight. We fear, we flee. But running from a fear generally gets us nowhere but tired. In some cases, that flight reaction can lead to denial of reality. When we are so afraid that we deny reality, then what we fear cannot happen. If it cannot happen, then we have nothing to fear. Therefore, we are safe.

In our work life, we run from problems in the same way. We pretend that they are not really problems; hence we can ignore them. Even the best adjusted of us has the ability to ignore problems in the hope that they will go away. So when our boss creates a fear that we will lose our jobs if we fail, one option is to assume that the boss really does not mean it and ignore the problem.

121

Another reason people freeze when confronted with fear is that they do not know what to do to succeed. They become immobilized and do nothing, not because they are trying to avoid work, but because they do not know what to do. They are afraid to take any action for fear it will create failure. Signs of this problem happening can range from staring out a window to absence from work for protracted periods.

Another type of reaction to fear can be a physical or mental shutdown. The body gets strong messages from the brain that something is wrong and reacts in a psychosomatic way and becomes ill. The medical community has in the recent past become acutely aware of the mind-body connection. The field of holistic medicine has emerged in recognition of the idea that emotional events such as intense fear can trigger very serious illness. These illnesses are not just in the mind. They are real, physical illnesses that can destroy a person. These reactions can range all the way from stress headaches to heart attacks, from rashes to severe immune system deficiencies.

In short, fear does work to push people, but leading by fear can have negative psychological and physiological impacts on associates. Why would a person who loves others create that type of "dis-ease"? Although punishment is sometimes necessary, it must be used sparingly and only when rewards fail to deliver results. Unfortunately, punishment frequently fails as well with people who have not responded to rewards.

At times punishment is the only option, but it always carries the risk of adverse reactions. When somebody makes a serious error, the first action may be negative feedback. As an example, if a machine operator endangers the life of a coworker or an error by a clerk could have resulted in a $1 million loss, negative feedback is obviously required, even though there is a reasonable risk of serious adverse consequences from the associate's reaction. No reasonable work leader could be expected to hold back from the emotional reaction of a first class scolding. The key to managing this negative feedback is to follow up with constructive corrective action. Turning a negative into a positive is a must if you want to provide a real developmental experience.

Sometimes You Have No Choice but to Be Negative

Every Leader has abandoned "rewards only" leadership more than once. At times, the only possible action is a negative action. It is natural to expect that you will get a negative reaction in return, so make certain that the advantages outweigh the impact of that negative reaction. Fear and anger, the natural reactions in response to a criticism, can energize or enervate. Assess the potential result if the associate has an unfavorable reaction to your negative feedback and decide if you can live with the consequences. As we said earlier, negative feedback probably is best reserved for times when you have had no real success with other attempts.

The real issue here is not always related to the situation or to the associate involved. It may also be related to your prior behavior. When a tough boss, with a reputation for being critical, gives a strong piece of negative feedback, it may simply be viewed as just another incident, or it may be viewed as one incident too many. On the other hand, when a normally mild-mannered, quietly positive leader turns negative, the change will probably be strong and full of surprise and dramatic influence.

123

Your associates will expect you to be upset when a truly horrible situation develops. Remember that if you do not identify a problem, you cannot help people improve themselves. For this reason, even though you want to focus on positive feedback, it is also essential that your associates understand where their weaknesses are. Negative feedback, or a focus on failure, is inevitably a part of even a positive approach to changing behavior. Do not recoil from identifying weaknesses just because you are trying to focus on the positive. In short, do not let the "be positive" message prevent you from getting the improvement your unit needs.

Rewards Will Reinforce Behavior—Good or Bad

Organizations do elicit the behavior they reward, whether the behavior is good or bad. Contain the negative impacts by making certain that your rewards, explicit and implicit, are focused on the behavior you view as good.

Let's consider a few simple examples. Imagine an organization that has an incentive system that rewards the sales and marketing departments by paying a flat commission on all sales over $1000. The range of pricing for the products is $500–$25,000. Let us also assume that the profit on a $25,000 item is thirty times greater than the profit on a $1,000 item. Obviously, the company would like to have the sales force sell as many large-ticket items as possible since it makes more money on them. Although the incentive structure will encourage sales over $1,000, we can be fairly certain that the staff will not pay much attention to selling items with a higher profit margin since the incentive offers no extra reward to them and $1,000 sales are likely to be easier. The company will encourage sales, but not the ones it really wants.

In another case, we can look at a company with an open-door policy for employees. Let's assume that employees are told that if they have a problem with their supervisor they always have the right, indeed are encouraged, to take the issue to the next higher level of management. Many very fine companies have such policies, and they can be quite effective at giving employees meaningful "escape valves" for legitimate supervisory problems.

In this example, the company has had the policy for three years and it seems to be working to everybody's satisfaction, except in one department. In this department, several supervisors have complained to the human resources department about the policy, saying that it substantially undercuts their ability to manage. The director of human resources is concerned and conducts an investigation. He finds that there are ten times as many complaints in that department as in any other in the company.

On further investigation, he discovers that when the department manager receives a complaint, he always overrules the supervisor. In other words, the complaint is always resolved in the employee's favor.

It is possible that the every supervisor in that department has a leadership problem; however, it is more likely that the manager has created the problem because he rewards each complaining employee by always agreeing with the complaint. Over time, employees in his department have realized that if they complain, they get their way; therefore, they should always complain.

As you can tell in each of these examples, it does not take long for the associates in an organization to "break the code." In the first instance, they figure out how to make the most money, and they use the easiest way to do that. In the second instance, they conclude that they can have anything they want just by making a complaint up the chain of command. The organizations elicited the behavior they rewarded. The only problem was that the behavior was undesired.

Ironically, the second example is the most frequent mistake leaders make. In the first instance, most organizations will put serious thought into such an incentive plan and it will, in all likelihood, be adjusted to encourage high-profit sales long before it is implemented. In the second instance, the policy probably has safeguards built in, but its execution is a leadership responsibility. The manager is rewarding undesired behavior in spite of a sound policy.

Leaders do this very often without recognizing the impact. We do it when we allow an unsatisfactory employee to continue in a job long past the time that we should have taken adverse action. We do it when we promote the wrong person. We do it when we allow a person to come in late almost every day without any disciplinary action. In each of these circumstances, we reward the wrong behavior by allowing it to continue. All associates get the message, and they will begin to exhibit the undesired behavior. Like it or not, all of our decisions are on stage.

For example, if your associates see promotions based on personal charisma of people whom they know to be lazy, they will conclude that the way to success is to be a nice person who goes home early. Much sooner than you might expect, you will see your entire staff race to the door at 4:30 p.m. every day.

It is important to give rewards for the right behavior with the right associates. Norm Augustine tells it this way: "Recognition of accomplishment (and the lack thereof) is an essential form of feedback. To reward poor performance or neglect outstanding performance is like placing the controls for each separate half of an electric blanket on the wrong side of the bed. Think about it."[30] If you do, it will be clear that such a leader is sending all the wrong signals to all the associates.

WORK LEADERS TIP

Watch Out for Misleading Rewards

Here are just a couple of examples of how the correct intent can lead to the wrong result.

__The intent__: To motivate an associate to increase throughput at the work station by providing an incentive to speed up production.

__The tactic:__ Tell an associate that he can go home just as soon as he finishes the assembly of the last twenty units on his work station.

__The result__: The associate speeds up the process and completes the units and leaves one hour early. The units have a defect rate that is three times that normally produced by the associate and five times that of the unit as a whole.

__The intent__: To improve the performance of a weak associate by offering an added incentive to meet the quality standards of the unit.

__The tactic:__ Tell the worst performing associate that if he achieves the customer service satisfaction standards that he will get a day off of his choosing.

__The result__: The associate achieves the improvement in performance and is rewarded with a day off. The best performing associate finds out about the reward and is incensed and insulted because he needs a day off to take an ailing child for tests but he has no more days left because they have all been *used to care for the child. He starts looking for another job because he thinks the company does not appreciate his work.*

Cash Always Has a Benefit, but Less Than You May Realize

Financial rewards are a positive reinforcement for behavior. In fact, most work leaders consider cash as king. Every survey ever done by researchers has financial rewards as a useful factor, but virtually no surveys provide conclusive evidence that they are the most important. When you look to reward associates, you will always have financial rewards in your quiver, but it cannot be the only arrow. That said, never ignore financial rewards. They matter, and they should be used when appropriate.

127

WORK LEADERS **TIP** When Using Financial Rewards, Use These Questions To Decide What To Do

- *Think about the last salary review you did and the conversation you had with your staff member. Was the salary increase a good increase by your standards? If so, did your staff member appreciate it? Did the salary increase actually reward performance? Did it encourage that person to do even better? Has that person done better since the increase was given?*

- *Does your organization have an incentive system that rewards top performers? How does it operate and how do you apply it to your staff? Has it worked to recognize performance? Has it worked to encourage performance?*

- *Make a list of the top five financial rewards that you plan to use during the next six months to reward performance.*

•*Do you believe that the associate whose performance you are going to reward is "money motivated"? How can you make that decision? What happened when you last gave that associate a merit raise? Have you ever used a financial or cash reward to reinforce behavior in that associate? How did it work?*

Catch Them Doing Something Right

When you house break a pet, the key to the training is to reward, or punish, behavior quickly. In the same way, you must catch your associates doing something right and reward them for it quickly. They too will remember the correct action a great deal better if the reward is on the spot, rather than substantially delayed. The same goes for errors. It makes no sense to give an admonishment six months later. Do it immediately.

In the United States, we are not a society focused on patiently waiting for long-term feedback. We tend to want our feedback immediately, not later. When we look for rewards, the same is true. Given this reality, we, as leaders, need to look for ways to reward positive behavior and results. Look for small rewards, as well as large ones. If a person you have coached on interpersonal skills comes to the office with a particularly pleasant demeanor and takes the time to be nice to a colleague, then you should take the time to reward that behavior, right then and there. If a sloppy worker does a particularly good job of cleaning up his workstation, reward him immediately. If a secretary you have coached about a lack of persistence finds a document that she has been searching for days to find, give her a reward right then. If a salesperson closes a sale that he needed to make his goal for the month, reward him. In every respect, catch your associates doing something right and reward them for it immediately. You will be amazed at the impact.

WORK LEADERS TIP   Plan for the Right Rewards

- *What is your plan to catch the correct behavior?*

- *Have you trained your associates to know what the right behavior is?*

- *Make a list of five non-financial rewards you will use to reward performance on the spot when you catch somebody doing something right.*

- *Make a list of each person in your unit and beside the names indicate what is most important to that person. On that same list, identify something you could do for or give to each individual as a reward for accomplishing a specific goal. Also list one thing that you think you could hold out to them to receive as an incentive reward for reaching a goal.*

- *Describe the one reward you have received that was the most powerful incentive for you to continue to perform at an exceptional level. Would it apply to anybody in your unit?*

- *Create a list of those programs that you would like to see your organization create so that you could use them to motivate or reward your staff. Make certain that at least half are programs that would have little or no money being given to the staff. Rank the list in order of your most desired.*

- *Write a detailed plan for getting your organization to implement one of the programs you listed.*

Use Praise, Not Just Money

How should you reward your associates? Remember that recognition is far more powerful than monetary rewards. Of course, it is important to pay people what they are worth, and often what they are worth changes as their performance improves. Compensation is not irrelevant, yet it has much less of an impact than most leaders expect. People will do almost the impossible if they think they are appreciated and if they are being led by a person who cares (loves).

Praise can be an art form or it can be a waste of time. When associates do the right thing or get the right result, they must know the leader noticed. But noticing is not enough. Be certain that you communicate that you approve of their performance and that you want them to continue to achieve that same success in the future. The real issue for a leader is to know when and how to reward.

Make certain that you pick the right time to reward. You should always find a way to reward for success when expectations are achieved. It is particularly important to reward those efforts that result in successes where failure existed before or when a major milestone has been achieved along an improvement plan. Always try to make the reward or praise happen right after the success.

WORK LEADERS TIP
Giving Rewards
Is Almost an Art Form

Cash rewards usually are effective rewards, but you will always be amazed at how effective non-cash rewards can be. Give an associate something that can be symbolic of a success and that can be seen and admired by others and you will almost always enhance the associates self esteem. Try some of these ideas:

A Few Examples of How and When

- A praising comment
- Flowers
- Candy
- A trip to Hawaii
- A note saying "Thank you"
- A phone call saying "Good work"
- Public approval
- Comments in a meeting about an achievement
- An e-mail containing praise, with a copy to the HR file
- A party in the persons honor
- A pizza party for the entire unit
- Lunch
- A cup of coffee at break time
- A visit to the person's desk to tell him, "Great job"
- A formal letter to the file noting extraordinary performance
- A handshake
- Some marketing material with the company logo, (i.e., pen, letter opener, sweater, tie)
- Golf balls for a golfer
- A formal, rotating trophy for Associate of the Month
- A certificate of appreciation framed for the wall in the person's workspace
- A $100 on-the-spot bonus for something extraordinary
- An item from the organization's formal recognition program

CASE STUDY

"Laura, I need to talk to you!"

These were words Laura had heard from her boss before. They always gave her a headache. Here we go again, she thought, another tongue-lashing.

Before Laura could see what Barbara wanted, the phone rang. She had been waiting for a callback from an irate customer and wanted to take the call. But given her boss's tone of voice, she decided to go see her first.

Barbara noticed Laura ignoring the call, and before Laura could say anything, she said, "You know how we all are trying to improve our customer service rankings. Letting that call go unanswered is clearly not great customer service. And that is what I want to talk to you about. I got another complaint call about you, this time on your phone etiquette. Laura, I cannot understand how this happens. I have talked to you about this problem several times in the last year, and you do not seem to get the message. The last time I put you on probation and gave you a thirty-day warning. That seemed to get your attention. But within another six months, you did it again. I am getting fed up with your inability to learn. What do you have to say for yourself?"

By now, Laura was beginning to have another one of those spells that her therapist called an anxiety attack. She was starting to feel weak, her breathing was becoming rapid, and she knew that soon she would start hyperventilating. The *fear was getting so severe that she felt she was going to pass out.*

Her boss looked at her and said, "What is wrong with you? You look awful."

Laura could barely catch her breath long enough to say, "I am having an attack. The doctors warned me about them. Please help!"

Barbara tried to calm her, but she kept getting whiter and whiter. Panicked, Barbara started shouting at people in the office to call 911. Fortunately, one of the associates, Carol, knew how to handle hyperventilation. Carol rushed to her desk, dumped her lunch out of a paper bag, and put it over Laura's mouth. After a few minutes, Laura began breathing more normally. The crisis seemed to have passed.

Barbara turned away and went back to her office. A couple of hours later, she came by and asked Laura how she was. "Oh, by the way, I got two letters complimenting you on your customer service today. I thought you might want them. I hope you feel better tomorrow."

133

Questions / Discussion Points

1. What is Laura's problem? Can she fix it herself?

2. Is Barbara a good leader? What defines her leadership?

3. Is Laura a problem for Barbara? What should Barbara do about Laura?

4. If Barbara is a problem, what should she do to be a better leader?

5. Did Barbara do well to give the letters to Laura? Did she get the maximum benefit from that act? How could she have used them better?

CHAPTER SEVEN

Self
Work Leaders Must Lead Themselves

This chapter is all about you. Every leader is a human being—an individual first, a leader second. This is not a chapter about being selfish. It is a discussion of how you must care for your "self" so that you will be able to give of that self to others. Your duty as a leader is to love your associates enough to make certain that you expect, assign, develop, evaluate and reward them and their performance on the job. You must give yourself the same—not a greater—priority if peak performance is your goal, you must be a leader to yourself. In the same way that you make certain that your associates fulfill their potential, so must you make certain that you fulfill your potential. You must evaluate your opportunities for improvement, work to develop yourself through effective evaluations of your performance, and have an improvement plan that gives structure to your efforts to develop yourself. The key here is to recognize that these steps to improvement are all interrelated and not always sequential. Dave Heenan, in *Double Lives* suggests,

> Cultivate the art of making yourself up as you go along. The process of rediscovery will expand your world. As Jean-Jacques Rousseau once put it, "The world of reality has its limits; the world of imagination is boundless."

Don't draw lines that limit what you are or are not. Doing so may eliminate novel invitations and the chance of switching gears. Don't edit out choices or become pigeonholed. Do be on a continuous hunt for what you love, what you do well, and what just piques your curiosity.[31]

Love: Self-Love Gives Us Strength and Confidence

The first core leader principle is that a leader must focus on loving the associates. Since this chapter is about you, then you must begin with a focus on loving yourself.

If we do love ourselves in a healthy way, then we feel a sense of peace with who we are. We know our strengths and weaknesses, our good qualities, and our faults, and we accept them. Indeed, our self-love allows us to forgive ourselves for our failings and allows us to reconcile those failings with our achievements. We are in balance because we are able to look past our human characteristics and accept ourselves as we are. Consider John Gardner's advice on how to renew yourself: "For self-renewing men and women the development of their own potentials and the process of self-discovery never end. It is a sad but unarguable fact that most people go through their lives only partially aware of the full range of their abilities."[32]

This love of self must not be confused with arrogance or conceit. Self-love allows us to recognize our human frailty and the need to constantly attempt to improve while at the same time it allows us to accept our self as we find it. This acceptance of our self allows us to be at peace with our existence and allows us to avoid the terrible pitfalls of self-pity, self-anger, and other self-inflicted wounds that invariably impact the way we relate to the rest of the world. For example, if you compare your knowledge, skills, and capabilities to others, you are likely to find an associate who outshines you in one or all of those categories. If you do not love yourself, you will probably be angry at being less capable than the individual you used as a benchmark comparison. That anger will eat away at your own self-concept, and in all likelihood, it will be directed at the benchmark individual. Hence, not loving yourself can ultimately cause you to be unable to love your associates.

After considering whether you love yourself, you must ask whether your associates love you. Put yourself in their shoes and ask the question, "If I were my leader, would I love the leader?" That takes a bit of objectivity and a great deal of honest, candid thinking on your part. Take the last week's worth of interactions with your team members and try to think through how you would have reacted to a boss who did what you did. Did you empathize at the right time? Did you criticize without constructive purpose? Did you listen to a complaint and then help the associate? Did you set an example in a time of crisis? Did you back off when you were wrong, or did you continue to try to prove you were right? In short, do you like the boss you see when you look in the mirror?

Of course, you can also go to your associates and attempt to determine directly from them how they feel. Such a poll can be very difficult to do on your own, but many organizations do climate or employee surveys with the objective of gaining a greater understanding of how leaders stand with their associates. You probably have experienced one of these in the past. How did you feel about it? Many bosses resist the results; however, they do so at their own peril. Sometimes, these kinds of surveys are the only effective way to get associates to tell you what they think you do not want to hear. Do not let self-absorption blind you from the truth of your associate's feedback.

137

If you are lucky, your organization might even have a 360-degree appraisal system where peers and subordinates get the opportunity to give you feedback. If so, treat this as an opportunity, not as a threat. You will be to learn a great deal about how people perceive you.

WORK LEADERS TIP
Do You Really Love Yourself?

Since we are not therapists, and since self-diagnosis is very difficult, what can we do to determine if we are comfortable with ourselves? Here are some questions you might want to ask yourself. The answers are yours. There are no right answers, no wrong answers.

- *When you get up in the morning, are you reluctant to go to work and deal with your associates?*

- *When you start a conversation with your boss, are you uneasy? Do you look forward to the meeting or do you put it off to the last minute?*

- *Do you dislike the feeling you have when your boss challenges an action you have taken?*

- *When an associate challenges your judgment, do you get defensive and argue with that person even if you know you were wrong?*

- *When you and your spouse or significant other are out dining and another man or woman looks with interest, does anxiety and even anger well up inside?*

- *When you look in the mirror, do you dislike what you see?*

- *When somebody gives you a compliment, do you have a hard time saying thank you?*

- *Are you jealous of anybody in your family? A friend?*

- *Do you have trouble being alone?*

If you answered yes to a majority of these questions, you may love yourself less than you should in order to be an effective Work Leader. You may need help feeling better about you!

138

EXPECTATIONS:
Set Expectations for Your Life and Career

Personal goal setting is an arduous task and one that is seldom completed. Our life plans are really a work in progress. Many of us at an early age were led, generally in a very sincere and loving way, by goals that our parents believed would be best for us. However, along with goals must come the desire to achieve them. You are the only person who can set your personal goals, and they must be a priority for you or they will end up being discarded scraps of paper tossed to the wind.

For some, an obsessive focus on a specific goal is the ticket to success and happiness. To others, obsessive focus, without the flexibility to respond to opportunity and changing personal conditions, is a ticket to frustration. Which applies to you may be a critical question; however, seldom does peak performance, hence peak career success, occur without an almost obsessive focus on goals the person has set. Reading the biographies of truly remarkable achievers will send one clear message to all who are willing to listen: commitment drives achievement. Make your goals your greatest priority and they will become your greatest joy. If your goals cannot command this level of focus and commitment, then you may have the wrong goals.

Remember, you must always be certain your goals are aligned with those of your organization and, if possible, with those of your boss. Alignment is essential because you cannot afford to go down a path that is out of step with your organization's focus. If you want to be an engineer and you work for an accounting firm, goal congruence will be difficult. If you want to be a CPA (certified public accountant) in the same firm, it is likely that you will find goal congruence and even organizational support for your goals. If you are caught in this conflict, solve it. Make certain that your job supports your goals. If it does not, change jobs. Your long-term goals must be a priority.

Your Expectations Must Be a Priority for You

The process of setting plans for your life is a subject much larger than the few pages we can devote to it. Literally thousands of very good books have been written to help people plan their lives, and we will not try to replicate their wisdom here. The sound advice can be boiled down to many of the same tools used for planning by organizations. Here are five steps for a career plan:

1. **SWOT**
2. **Long-term Goals/Objectives**
3. **Strategies**
4. **Tactical Goals**
5. **Action Plans**

SWOT

A SWOT (strengths, weaknesses, opportunities, and threats) analysis forms the basis for a sound plan, whether organizational or individual. Knowing your strengths and weaknesses is essential to making life and career decisions that you will actually be able to carry out. Unrealistic goals that assume strengths you do not have can spell disaster. Knowing your life or career opportunities and the threats you face is essential to knowing what the future might hold. It would be foolish to plan to be a leader of a railroad company if you think that jobs in that industry are going to disappear, and it might be tragic if you failed to become trained in mathematics and computer science if you think that is where the preponderance of job growth is going to be. In short, looking at these four factors can help you understand what career might be a correct match for you.

Long-Term Goals

If you do not have a long-term plan, you are making a terrible mistake. You cannot leave the next twenty years of your life to chance. If you do have such a plan, it will force you to take steps to make certain you are ready for the future. You may never achieve the goal you had in mind, but all the evidence is that if you are focused on it, you have a much better chance of getting there. Once again, if you want to be a CPA, then taking courses in accounting can further that goal. Courses in art history may be fun, or even an important contribution to your general development, but they will probably not help you achieve your career goal of being a professional accountant.

Strategies

Strategies are tough but essential. They will cause you to think about the key decisions you are going to need to make in order to achieve those long-term goals. You may decide that a job change is essential; you may decide a major educational enhancement is required, or you may decide to move to another city or state. You may also decide that you will start down a new career path in order to get yourself ready for the next stage of your life.

141

Tactical Goals

Tactical goals are shorthand for short-term goals—those that you are going to set in motion this week, this month, or this year. They can be as complex as "Get a new job" or as uncomplicated as "Make my sales goal for the month." Whatever the goal, it should not only fit into the larger scheme of your life but also be something that you can achieve for your personal benefit and career.

Action Plans

Action plans are what you are going to do today, tomorrow, or next week to achieve those goals, either long or short-term. This is where the Work Leader in you should shine. You are an action person and you must achieve these goals.

All of the five above steps suggest that you should apply the techniques you use as a work leader to help you reach your personal life goals as well. If you do, linking the personal goals with your Work Leader goals will be a lot easier.

Your career is yours to accept or to create. You must ignore the conventional wisdom and the conventional view of previous career models. John Kotter, in *Leading Change* suggests,

> For a lot of reasons, many people are still embracing the 20th century career and growth model. Sometimes complacency is the problem. They have been successful, so why change? Sometimes they have no clear vision of the 21st century, and so they don't know how they should change. But often fear is a key issue. They see jobs seeming to disappear all around them. They hear horror stories about people who have been downsized or reengineered out of work. They worry about health insurance and the cost of college for their children. So they don't think about growth. They don't think about personal renewal. They don't think about developing whatever leadership potential they have. Instead they cling defensively to what they currently have. In effect, they embrace the past, not the future.[33]

Assignment: Make Certain You Are Assigned to a Job That Allows Achievement

Just as you need to establish a disciplined process for assigning associates to the right job, so must you focus on your own assignment. Nothing is more disabling than a bad assignment. On one hand, the psychological impact of job unhappiness are well known and may even be underestimated. You spend more time at the workplace than at any other activity. All work generates some stress, and responsible positions can generate high stress levels. If you are miserable, the added stress that builds can have a devastating impact on your mind and on your physical health as well. These impacts show up not just at work, but also in the remainder of your life as well.

In the event that you are in an incorrect assignment, then you are likely to be damaging your career. Being assigned to the wrong job is no less a problem in your career than it is for your associates in their careers. Always make certain that your assignment is a good fit for you. How do you know if an assignment is a good fit? The best way is to know your strengths and weaknesses and how those relate to any given position. This is no simple task. It is not easy for most of us to objectively evaluate ourselves. We either do not want to really know our own weaknesses or we have a tendency to always view our weaknesses as some type of strength.

When you are evaluating whether a new position is a good fit from your perspective, you must be certain to be honest with yourself. If you happen to be impatient, and you know that patience is truly a requirement for the job, then do not allow yourself to take on the assignment without understanding how you will deal with this shortcoming. Otherwise, you are likely to find yourself in trouble quickly. The trouble will either be a failure to perform or physical health problems because of the added stress from working at a job that is a bad fit.

You must also consider, even if you can you do the job, whether it is one that truly fulfills you. This aspect may have much less disastrous short-term consequences to your career, but it can be terribly stressful nonetheless.

143

What should you do if you find yourself in a job that is a bad fit? Get out of the mismatch. In the short run, you may be able to do the job, but in the long run you are probably going to lose the ability to achieve peak performance. Get out while you still are excited about your work. Once that is gone, the boss will notice and you will be at risk.

The key point here is let go of the past. Make certain you are prepared to leave a job that is wrong for you. There is no substitute for job satisfaction from a job that fulfills a long-term goal. As Spencer Johnson says in his best-selling book, *Who Moved My Cheese?* "The quicker you let go of old cheese, the sooner you find new cheese."[34]

WORK LEADERS TIP

Are You in the Right Job?

To find out if you are in the wrong job, ask these questions. Do you

- *Hate to go to work in the morning?*
- *Find Monday your worst day of the week? Is Friday, your best day?*
- *Dislike your fellow associates?*
- *Dislike your boss?*
- *Get tired during the day?*
- *Wish you could find another job?*
- *Take your break every day at exactly the same time?*
- *Get home totally exhausted and uninterested in talking about work?*
- *Leave work exactly on time every day?*
- *Find every excuse to not go to work?*

Development: Provide For Your Own Development

Lifelong learning has been a popular concept in academic circles for a long time, yet the reality of its application to the work world has been recent. Too many leaders have completed their formal education and then assumed that they knew all they needed to succeed. The 1990s proved otherwise as thousands of employees throughout corporate America found themselves downsized and outplaced. Many of them were highly paid middle managers with knowledge and skills limited largely to what was required by their previous jobs.

As these leaders found, the pace of change in the world had accelerated to such a phenomenal rate that within a decade they had fallen behind. And the rate of change will continue to accelerate even further. Anybody entering the work force today will face the prospect of several different careers during a lifetime. This prospect can be either frightening or exciting, depending on how people prepare for the change. Those who choose to be leaders will also need to choose to renew and reinvent themselves several times during their working career. Lifelong learning is essential to survival in the new millennium.

Individual Development: Improve or Fall Behind!

The Japanese have a word for this concept: Kaizen, which means continuous improvement. From the book, *Kaizen:* "The essence of Kaizen is simple and straightforward: Kaizen means improvement. Moreover, Kaizen means ongoing improvements involving everyone, including both managers and workers. The Kaizen philosophy assumes that our way of life—be it our working life, our social life, or our home life deserves to be constantly improved."[35] A commitment to this core principle is the heart of the Total Quality revolution that swept through the manufacturing sector during the last decade. In the United States, we have almost always had a strong bias toward innovation and breakthrough thinking. No doubt this is at the heart of much of the success we have had in leading the world of change, but the concept of continuous improvement added a significant dimension to the production equation. Instead of a focus on hitting home runs every day, the Kaizen approach calls for tiny little improvements that add up to significant change. When we in the United States began to combine our capacity for innovation with that of continuous improvement, we managed not only to catch up to the Japanese companies, but we began to pass them.

The same concept must hold true for us as individuals. We must continue to focus on major breakthroughs in learning, but we must also deploy continuous improvement through daily learning. The breakthroughs can be as small as completing a single distance learning course on television or as large as completing a master's degree program. Continuous learning can be as complex as learning a new processing system being implemented at work or as simple as learning about a new Intel chip that has more processing speed.

145

New knowledge is essential if we are to keep up with the pace of change, and we must look for it in many different places. By continuously learning, you are investing in yourself. Almost all of us have some type of investment program. We put away capital for the future and that is a very wise move; however, how many of us have a firm plan to invest some of our savings in our own development?

One of the best ways to learn is to take advice—wherever you can get it. The smartest people are always asking questions. We all have something to learn from others. For some, the thought of asking a question is an admission that they do not know something. For others, asking a question is the start of an exploration of ideas. Instead of always giving your opinions about issues, try asking others for theirs.

Thinking "outside the box" is a very popular concept, but you will probably find it is almost impossible to do alone because sometimes our own minds are the box we are trapped in. It can be extremely useful to have somebody else state a point or ask a question that you would not even have thought about.

Find a Mentor, Be a Mentor, and Make Certain There Is Love

Much has been said recently about mentoring, but its value cannot be overstated. Some of my most important learning came from a mentor. One in particular, who happened along at the start of my corporate career, was critical to helping me find my way. He gave me tough jobs, tough advice, tough critiques, and tough rules, but he was kind, warm, and caring. He loved me, and I knew it. He was there when I needed him and was silent when it was best for me to work through the issue on my own. I could ask him for advice, I could argue with him or I could simply sit and listen while he shared his philosophy of leadership and life. I did not always agree with him; I did not always like what he said; I did not always agree with what he did, but I always loved him as my mentor.

He found a way to cover for me when I made my mistakes. He protected me while at the same time helping me to learn how I could avoid repeating the same mistake. He influenced me and helped me to grow at a rate much faster than had I been alone. He pushed me to achieve more than I ever dreamed possible.

I was lucky to have been found by my mentor, and I made a promise to myself that whenever I had the chance, I would do for others what had been done for me. I never really looked for somebody to mentor; I simply kept my eyes open for unique talent that was worth investing in. Mentoring takes more than time. I knew that my mentor had given a great deal of himself to help me, and I wanted to be certain that his investment in me would enable me to help others fulfill their true potential.

Being a mentor is not just psychologically rewarding, it is an enormous growth opportunity as well. When you choose to help another, you will be amazed at how much you will learn from your mentee. In the beginning the relationship that develops in the beginning is like that of a parent and child, but as the relationship matures, its nature changes, until ultimately it is that of adult and adult. When you arrive at this mature stage, you will find the greatest learning occurs for both of you. In addition, knowing that you have had a material impact on the life of a truly gifted person is very rewarding. Continue to search for new mentees, and you will be richly rewarded as well.

147

Take All the Training You Can

Assuming you work for an organization that believes in training, grab all of the training they will pay for. If it isn't offered, volunteer to take it. If the training you are given is bad, help the organization make it better. If you work for an organization that pinches pennies on training, then you must either attempt to get the organization to change or change organizations.

The specific type of training you take at your organization is critical. Some organizations focus on technical training for leaders. If you work for such an organization, then make certain that you get all the technical training available. You cannot work in such an organization if the leadership thinks that you are not technically competent. Other organizations believe that the key skills for their leaders are managerial and/or administrative. The same core advice holds: get the kind of training the organization wants.

In any case, you will have to go far beyond organizational training. True, some organizations will pay for part or all of a formal degree program and some will even send you to a full time training or educational experience. However, you are going to need further development. That will be a serious demand on your time. Whether you decide to get a master's degree, professional certification, law degree, or some other advanced recognition, you will need to commit substantial time and financial resources to that effort. Do not hesitate.

Invest in yourself. Even if the organization has a tuition reimbursement program, you will need to spend money and time on this commitment. Most evening masters of business administration programs will take two or more years of classes at night. Make the commitment, not because you are going to get a raise, but because it will help you survive the chaos of a changing world. Indeed, most organizations do not even give adequate recognition for these efforts until well past the time that you completed the work.

The credential is not the most critical aspect of a degree program. The value lies in two places: (a) the knowledge, skills, and attitudes gained from the coursework and (b) the colleague contacts made during the program. These contacts may never get you a promotion or a new job, but you will also be learning from them. The dynamics of hearing and seeing people from other organizations are invaluable.

Remember, not all development is schooling and training programs. Just plain reading may be the best way to develop yourself. Read everything and anything you find interesting or useful in your chosen field and elsewhere. If you are in business, read the *Wall Street Journal*, business management books, and read business magazines, as well as novels, and books about technology, the arts, and politics. In short, learn all you can about a wide range of issues that have even a marginal relationship to your work. This breadth of learning will pay dividends as you compete for the next promotional opportunity. It will improve your understanding of the world about you and position you to take on added and higher responsibilities that are impacted by more than the immediate work you are currently leading.

Also participate in outside activities such as sports, hobbies, the theater, and so on. All of these offer you not only the opportunity to get away from the daily grind of work, but they also offer a chance to network with others who might someday be a part of your career life. Volunteer in a variety of organizations and meet people outside of your current career field. Indeed, you may someday find that those contacts will help you to redirect your career. By knowing others, you also get to know other professions as well. All of these activities contribute to your development not just as a professional but also as a more complete person.

Evaluation: Evaluate Yourself

If you are getting little constructive evaluation or feedback on your performance, what alternatives do you have? You cannot develop yourself if you have no idea how you need to improve. Evaluation is intended to offer your associates and, in this case, you that insight. How many times have you received a performance review that really had an impact on you? Probably very seldom.

149

Try Your Boss First

Consider simply asking your boss for feedback. The worst that could happen is that she will say no. More likely she will dodge and weave but ultimately give you at least some type of evaluation. You may not like what you hear, but that is what you need to know. If you do get some troubling news, then you will have some advanced warning that your job may be at risk. This is a real possibility that happens every day in the world of work. Your goal should be to avoid the ultimate surprise of being terminated for failure when you thought that you were doing a great job. Find a way to get feedback that can help you improve since it might also save your job.

A more likely scenario for your attempt to get an evaluation from a reluctant boss is for you to hear, "Oh, everything is great. Just keep up the great work!" This is actually your worst-case scenario because in all likelihood it is simply not the truth. The comments may be well intended, but they are not enough. You need to be given the constructive criticism or compliments that will help you improve. The "everything is great" answer only makes you feel good about everything and that means not one positive behavior was reinforced and not one negative behavior was punished. In short, you got nothing but a comment that made you and your boss feel good about her failure to communicate. Keep trying; but this boss is unlikely to give you much more.

Most bosses who are reluctant to give feedback are eventually forced by the organization to do something, but if that process fails, then try writing your own appraisal. How to do that is another question. A good place to start is the performance review forms that your organization uses. Fill out a formal review of yourself using that form. Put yourself in your boss's shoes. Write the review based on what you think her perceptions are, not what you believe to be truth. Most of us know that others have different perceptions than we have, and we are usually convinced that those perceptions are in error. They are not. Like it or not, your boss's perception is reality for her. Your view is reality for you, but it is irrelevant. When she talks to you, when she talks to others, when she thinks about your performance or potential, she will base those conclusions and comments on her perceptions, not yours.

Perception is important because we all work in a world that is based on what others believe about us. If their perceptions are different from our view of the truth, then either we are wrong or their perception is wrong. In either case, the disparity between the two must be eliminated. Either we must change their view of us, or we must change our own self-view. Usually you will benefit more from accepting the boss's perception and attempting to correct or improve your performance.

Self-evaluation is tough to do and will take some practice to get it right. The irony is that once you take it seriously, you will be more critical of your performance than others might be. Once you begin, this process will be very therapeutic. Start now, and put in motion the forces for improvement. Your best improvement will come from responding to your most significant challenge.

How will you know what you should focus on first or most? The answer is to focus on the observation that is the hardest to accept, the one you are least able to look at objectively. If it truly is the most painful, then it is probably the most significant, deep-seated issue. Starting there can make the largest difference.

Have Others Who Love You Give You Feedback

Once you have given yourself a thorough look, you should then begin the painful process of asking others around you. If your organization has a 360-degree system, that will help, but what you really want is to have peers and subordinates alike feel comfortable enough with you to tell you what they perceive your strengths and weaknesses to be. However, you must be ready for almost any comments. Some will tell you only, "You're great." Others will tell you only what they know you want to hear. Still others will hint in some small way about a weakness, saying it is really nothing significant. Some will flatten you with criticism. Try to be calm and receptive. Of course, if one of your weaknesses is that you cannot accept criticism, then that will be very difficult.

151

Feedback from associates and peers can have almost more significance than that from a boss. If you are doing a good job in your current assignment, you are likely to get positive feedback from your boss. If, however, you are doing a great job at the expense of your relationships with peers or associates, you might be creating an environment where your current boss thinks you are great and everybody else in the organization is unhappy with you.

Keep in mind, you must carefully choose which colleagues to ask for feedback. Getting a friend to tell you what you want to hear may feed your ego, but it will not help you focus on those areas you should be addressing. Also, asking people who do not know your boss's expectations, no matter how objective they might be, may lead you to erroneous conclusions, no matter how sincere the feedback.

Focus on Your Weaknesses

Every self-help book advises you to be a positive thinker. It's true; we need to always feel good about ourselves. The fact is, however, our self-concept can be great, and we can be ineffective. One leader who had enormous self-esteem had achieved very significant stature in his organization. The problem: he saw no faults in himself and only weaknesses in the people around him. He trusted no one and he loved no one. Worse still, nobody could get close enough to him to say what he needed to hear. Eventually, he and the company failed. To this day, he says that he did not fail, but circumstances caused the failure. But he did fail. His ability to lead was impaired by his inability to love his associates and be realistic about himself.

Keep your positive self-esteem, but recognize that *everybody* can improve. Recognize your strengths and be certain that you continue to behave in ways that maximize their impact on yourself and your associates. However, focus also on those areas where you need improvement. This is positive, not negative thinking. Your thought process must be, I am good today, and I am going to be better tomorrow. I am positive that I will improve!

Make the Improvement Plan a Priority

Thinking you will improve and actually improving are quite different. Positive thinking must be turned into positive action. You must be energized to accomplish something. Without a plan of action and the resolve to act, you will achieve no predictable change and certainly will have no way of knowing if you are on course.

But what is a self-improvement plan? Where do you start and what does it look like? It starts with a decision that you understand the areas requiring attention. That means you must have an evaluation that you believe in. It may have come from a boss, from a peer or friend, or from within yourself. Whatever the case, you must believe that these areas really need your attention, and you must decide that you will set goals to address the weakness.

If you accept the conclusion that you have a weakness in financial analysis, for example, then you must set goals that will help you to develop the technical skills required to get better at that discipline. If that means taking courses, then you need to set a firm date when you will start the course. If you need help with the communication skills required to be an effective coach, then you need to determine the best way to get those skills. It may mean attending a seminar or it may require reading a few books and then following a disciplined practice program that either gives you role-playing experience with a friend or real work situations in which you use your newfound skills.

Whatever the case, you must establish a need, set a goal, set a specific strategy to achieve the new skills, and then set a date by which you will achieve the developmental experience required to improve your performance. Most importantly of all, write all of this down so that you can see the plan in real terms. People tend to remember information that impacts multiple senses. Seeing your goals in writing adds to your intellectual and emotional commitment to the plan.

153

No plan is worth the paper it is written on if all you do is put it in a file and leave it for another day. The plan belongs in your daily planner. It should be a to-do list item every day. It must influence your priorities in the same way that getting the work out affects every day at the job. If you do not treat your own development with the same priority that you give to your job, then you will always be a second-class citizen in your world. At a minimum, you must make your own development equally as important as that of your associates. Therefore, you must have a follow-up program that keeps the discipline of improvement at the forefront of your attention.

Every plan element must have a completion date, but just as importantly, each must also have intermediate checkpoints that provide you with frequent insight into how you are progressing. These progress checks are essential largely because without them the crush of day-to-day priorities will limit your improvement efforts unless you resist. At a minimum, every week you should check your performance against your plan. If you are falling behind, you should not wait for six months to go by to decide that you have failed to keep the commitment.

Rewards: Reward Your Own Success

So far, leading yourself has been hard work. Your natural reaction will be to say, "All this work deserves a reward." You must resist rewarding hard work. Never allow yourself to fall into the trap of confusing efforts with results. An improvement plan is great and you should feel good about getting to that stage, but feeling good is not enough. Reward yourself only when you achieve a goal.

The whole concept of self-reward assumes that you know how to deny yourself what you want. Perhaps the most significant difficulty in applying your LEADERS strategy to yourself is the issue of discipline. When you apply these concepts to your associates, you are the person in power. You control the leadership efforts, and you also control the final reward. You can give rewards when you think they are deserved, and you can deny them when you believe that an associate has fallen short. Rewarding yourself, on the other hand, requires you to play two roles—the "rewarder" and the "rewardee." This requires significant personal discipline. You must deny yourself a reward until you have a real achievement. If a reward is truly something you want, it will take great will and commitment to avoid cheating. If you resist, the reward will have a twofold benefit. First, you will reward the improvement in behavior you have been targeting. Second, you will reinforce personal discipline, which is itself a major behavioral characteristic that will pay huge dividends throughout your career and life. What a bargain: two lessons in one.

Be certain to keep the rewards in perspective. Make certain you save the big rewards for big accomplishments. A trip to Hawaii should be saved for a major milestone (like completing a full degree program, not just finishing a single course). This point may seem obvious, but it is easy to fall into this trap. What will you do for the really big accomplishment if the small ones get huge rewards? Unless you inherited a multimillion-dollar fortune, you will quickly run out of carrots and have only the discipline stick to keep you focused on big improvements.

You will find that the joy of achievement can itself become a powerful reward. In addition, you will become conditioned to continuous improvement as a way of life, rather than as an event you must force-feed yourself. This will happen in large part because you will continue to see improvement in your life and your career as you follow your development plan.

The other side of this process is punishment. You will generally have an easier time developing punishment systems for your associates than you will for yourself. This is because of the discipline factor. How do you punish yourself? Does punishment mean giving yourself pain or does it mean denial of something you want?

You may feel a need to punish yourself when you fail, but you must focus on what you will do to avoid the next mistake or failure in the future, not on the failure itself. Even if you can create a punishment that hurts you enough to motivate you to angry, getting angry has value only if it motivates you to take action to rectify the cause of the failure. Anger that is not directed toward constructive action often turns into remorse, regret, or self-pity. None of these will contribute to your achievement of a goal.

Regret is a useless burden. Mistakes are to be learned from. Learn to forgive yourself and to use your mistakes as stories to tell years from now. Use the mistake today as a basis for forming a new goal and a new plan to achieve your intended improvement and make certain you avoid making the same mistake once again.

The only effective way to follow up on a success is with a reward; the only effective way to follow up on a failure is to set a new goal and achieve it. Punishing yourself does not work any better than punishing your associates.

- *Do you know anybody who has had the problem of being passed over for a promotion? What happened to that person? Have you ever been passed over for a promotion you wanted? Why did that happen?*

- *Sometimes we never find out about a promotion we might have had. If you answered no the question above, how do you know that you did not lose a promotion without even knowing you were being considered?*

- *If you have been in your current job for five years or more, is there anything you should be doing to prepare for your next job? Has the organization given you any hints about what you should do?*

- *If you have been in your job for less that a couple of years, does the company have a plan for you? Does it fit your expectations? If it does, are you ready to move to the next job? If not, what do you need to do to get ready?*

- *Have you done a SWOT analysis on yourself? If not, prepare the analysis and then ask yourself what you have learned. Show the analysis to somebody you like and whose judgment you trust and ask that person to evaluate it.*

- *What is your long-term goal? Where do you want your life to be in ten years? In twenty years? Is there a match between your life goals and the career track you are on? If there is a divergence, what can you do to bring these two together?*

- *What are you going to do tomorrow to help you achieve your goals for the next year? What about next week? Develop a list of at least ten action plans for next week.*

CASE STUDY

Jamie had just lost her job and still didn't know why. She had worked for Chris for fifteen years and had always done everything she was asked to do. She had completed every project on time. Success for the organization was always her first priority. During all of those years, Jamie never once refused an assignment, no matter how much she was tempted.

Chris was a great boss, but last week she shocked everybody by resigning to take a job with a competitor. Since that time, Jamie had been a bit nervous about getting a new boss. After working for the same person for so long, Jamie knew that she would have a big adjustment, but she had always been able to succeed in the past so she was confident that she would do just fine.

Yesterday, her new boss, Michael, came to the office and had a talk with each of the members of the management team. When he got to Jamie, she got the shock of a lifetime. He was changing the organization and her job was being eliminated. He told her that since she had been there for so many years, she would get another job with the company, but right now he had no idea what it would be. Michael sent Jamie to Human Resources. Jamie's representative told her that there really was no job at the same level in the organization and that if Jamie wanted to remain with the company, she would need to step down to a lower position, maybe not even a supervisory role.

Jamie went home that night exhausted and depressed. She got into bed at 8:00 and fell asleep by 8:30. Unfortunately, she woke up at 11:00 and could not go back to sleep for almost the entire night. Jamie's life was in crisis, and she had no idea what to do. Life as Jamie knew it was over and she had no idea why.

Questions

1. Why is Jamie in this position?

2. Was Chris a good boss? What could she have done to help Jamie?

3. What should Jamie have done? When should she have done it?

4. Did Michael treat Jamie fairly? What should he have done?

5. What can Jamie do now? Is it too late for her?

6. If you were counseling Jamie, what would you suggest she do?

Revisited
From Love To Self

Our journey began with understanding the role of love in setting the tone of the relationship with your associates and concluded with a focus on creating a positive self-concept and being a leader to yourself. Between committing to honing your capacity to love associates and the role of loving and leading yourself you must set expectations, make a correct assignment, focus on development, provide effective evaluation, and deliver timely rewards. These leadership practices are necessary to foster, encourage, and assure peak performance from your associates. However, the real intensity of your efforts must be on yourself.

The role of leader places a burden on you that cannot be treated lightly. When you were an individual performer, your capacity to deliver results was the true measure of your success. As a work leader, you will probably continue to do tasks that generate results for your organization, but your true measure of success shifts dramatically. You must help your associates achieve success as individuals and as a team. You must not allow the term Work Leaders confuse you. You are not leading the work; you are leading the workers.

Your role is entirely new since now you must get your greatest happiness from the success of others rather than from your own. This is not a selfless act. It is quite self-focused. As a Work Leader, your only avenue to success is for your unit to succeed. Having a staff to lead means that the organization believes more than one associate is required to achieve the unit goals; hence you alone cannot achieve success. Your staff's pain of failure or excitement at success must be yours. Your goal must be to help staff members stay focused on the goals because their achievements will be your achievement.

The most effective way for your associates to grow and succeed is to learn from you. Once you are the Work Leader, you are the guiding light. You must be a bright beacon guiding them to achieve. Unfortunately, most of us are not ready for that role and responsibility. Few of us ask for it. Being the appointed leader usually comes to us because we were good at doing the work, not because we were groomed to lead.

We have focused on the seven essential steps required of an effective Work Leader. We have tried to emphasize the simplicity of the concepts, but the actual tasks of leading are tough work. Just as you needed to be trained to do your previous work assignment as an individual performer, so must you be given the boost required to develop the skills of a leader. There are few shortcuts to this development, and although most organizations recognize the challenge, few have discovered the secret of developing peak performance work leaders. All too often, as in our example earlier in the book, work leaders are "thrown into the water" to sink or swim with no real swimming lessons. Most Work Leaders tend to "doggy paddle" their way to survival, but many never learn to swim. They simply learn to avoid drowning. Are you one of those?

Just as in the case of a child, the only rational way to learn how to swim is to be taught by a person who has the knowledge and skills. The best way to learn how to lead is to work for a great leader, but if you are one who has been left to "sink or swim," we recommend you take action immediately. Find a great work leader, and then find a way to get into that unit. The payback will be enormous. Armed with the seven essential steps for Work Leader success, you will have the knowledge to develop the skills and attitudes you will need to learn to swim.

You need to become the great Work Leader that all associates want to work for. When that happens, you will have made the transition from Worker to Work Leader.

Just as importantly, once you have gained the skills required to be a great work leader, then it will be your turn to pass on your knowledge, skills, and attitudes to your associates. The reason is simple: somebody in your unit will probably some day be asked to step into your shoes as work leader. One of those associates is probably working for you because she wants to learn from a great work leader. Because you love them all, you owe it to all your associates to help your successor be more ready than you were.

BIBLIOGRAPHY

Chapter 1
Love—Friends Like but Leaders Love

Bennis, Warren and David A. Heenan. *Co-Leaders*. New York: John Wiley and Sons, 1999.

Bennis, Warren. *On Becoming a Leader*. Reading: Addison-Wesley, 1989.

Collins, James C. and Jerry I. Porras. *Built To Last*. New York: Harper Business, 1994.

DePree, Max. *Leadership is an Art*. New York: Doubleday, 1989.

Gardner, John W. *On Leadership*. New York: The Free Press, 1990.

Gellerman, Saul W. *Management by Motivation*. New York: American Management Association, 1968.

Kotter, John P. *The Leadership Factor*. New York: The Free Press, 1988.

Kotter, John P. *What Leaders Really Do*. Boston: Harvard Business Review Book, 1999.

Levinson, Harry. *The Exceptional Executive: A Psychological Conception*. Cambridge: Harvard University Press, 1968.

Levinson, Harry. *The Great Jackass Fallacy*. Boston: Division of Research Graduate School of Business Administration Harvard University, 1973.

Maxwell, John C. *The Twenty-One Irrefutable Laws of Leadership: Follow them and People Will Follow You*. Nashville: Thomas Nelson, 1998.

McGregor, Douglas. *The Human Side of Enterprise*. New York: McGraw Hill, 1960.

Ouchi, William G. *Theory Z*. New York: Avon Publishers, 1981.

Potter, Beverly A. *Changing Performance on the Job*. New York: American Management Associations Publications Group, 1980.

Chapter 2
Expectations—Setting the Bar Sets the Tone

Allen, Louis A. *Making Managerial Planning More Effective*. New York: McGraw-Hill, 1982.

Augustine, Norman R. *Augustine's Laws*. New York: Viking Penguin, 1968.

Crosby, Philip B. *Quality Is Free*. New York: McGraw-Hill, 1979.

Drucker, Peter R. *Management*. New York: Harper and Row, 1973.

Goldratt, Eliyahu M. *The Goal*. Croton-on-the Hudson: North River Press, 1992.

Grove, Andrew S. *High Output Management*. New York: Random House, 1983.

Machiavelli, Nicolo. *The Prince*. New York: The New American Library of World Literature, 1952.

Tichy, Noel M. and Sherman, Stratford. *Control Your Destiny or Someone Else Will*. New York: Currency Doubleday, 1993.

Chapter 3
Assignment—Square Pegs in Round Holes Never Fit!

Buckingham, Marcus and Curtis Coffman. *First Break All The Rules*. New York: Simon and Schuster, 1999.

Champy, James. *Reengineering Management*. New York: Harper Collins, 1995.

Collins, James C. *Good to Great—Why Some Companies Make the Leap...and Other's Don't*. New York: Harper Collins, 2002.

Fear, Richard A. *The Evaluation Interview*. New York: McGraw-Hill, 1978.

Jick, Todd D., Rosabeth Moss Kanter, and Barry A. Stein. *The Challenge of Organizational Change*. New York: The Free Press, 1992.

Lorsch, Jay W. and Thomas J. Tierney. *Aligning the Stars*. Boston: Harvard Business School Press, 2002.

Mintzberg, Henry. *The Structuring of Organizations*. Englewood Cliffs: Prentice-Hall, 1979.

Chapter 4
Development—The Good Get Better, the Best Excel!

Byham, William C., Ph.D. *Zapp! The Lightening of Empowerment*. New York: Harmony Books, 1988.

Connellan, Thomas K. *How to Improve Human Performance*. New York: Harper and Row, 1978.

Drucker, Peter F. *The Frontiers of Management*. New York: Truman Talley Books, 1986.

Gordon, Thomas, Dr. *Leader Effectiveness Training*. Solana Beach: Wyden Books, 1977.

Harry, Mikel and Schroeder, Richard. *Six Sigma*. New York: Doubleday, 2000.

Imai, Masaaki. *Kaizen*. New York: Random House Business Division, 1986.

Johnson, Harold, E. *Mentoring*. Glendale: Griffin Publishing Group, 1997.

Kotter, John, P. *Leading Change*. Boston: Harvard Business School Press, 1986.

Senge, Peter M. *The Fifth Discipline The Art and Practice of The Learning Organization*. New York: Doubleday, 1990.

Chapter 5
Evaluation—Leaders Succeed by Making Judgments

Batten, Joe D. *Tough-Minded Leadership*. New York: AMACOM, 1989.

Conner, Daryl R. *Managing At the Speed Of Change*. New York: Villard Books, 1993.

Covey, Stephen R. *Principle-Centered Leadership*. New York: Simon and Schuster, 1991.

Covey, Stephen R. *The 7 Habits of Highly Effective People*. New York: Simon and Schuster, 1989.

McConkey, Dale D. *How to Manage By Results*. New York: AMACOM, 1983.

Ogawa, Morimasa. *Pana-Management*. Tokyo: PHP Institute, 1991.

Peters, Thomas J. and Waterman, Robert H. *In Search of Excellence: Lessons from America's Best Run Companies*. New York: Harper and Rowe, 1981.

Shorris, Earl. *The Oppressed Middle, Politics of Middle Management*. Garden City: Anchor Press/Doubleday, 1981.

Wheatley, Margaret J. *Leadership and The New Science*. San Francisco: Berrett-Koehler Publishers, 1992.

Chapter 6
Rewards—An Organization Elicits the Behavior It Rewards

Austin, Nancy A. and Tom A. Peters. *Passion for Excellence*. New York: Random House, 1985.

Blanchard, Kenneth, Ph.D., Patricia Zigarmi, Ed.D. and Drea Zigarmi, Ed.D. *Leadership and the One Minute Manager*. New York: William Morrow, 1985.

Guaspari, John. *I Know It When I See It*. New York: AMACOM, 1985.

Haigh, Tim and Hanan, Mack. *Outperformers*. New York: AMACOM, 1989.

Matusushita, Konosuke. *Velvet Glove, Iron Fist*. Tokyo: PHP Institute, 1991.

Peters, Tom. *Liberation Management*. New York: Alfred A. Knopf, 1992.

Chapter 7
Self—Work Leaders Must Lead Themselves

Bossidy, Larry and Ram. Charan. *Execution*. New York: Crown Business, 2002.

Clavell, James. *The Art of War, Sun Tzu*. New York: Delacorte Press, 1983.

Cox, Allen. *The Making of the Achiever*. New York: Dodd, Meade, 1984.

Drucker, Peter F. *Managing In Turbulent Times*. New York: Harper and Row Publishers, 1980.

Gardner, John W. <u>Self-Renewal</u>. New York: W.W. Norton, 1995.

Heenan, David A. *Double Lives, Crafting Your Life Work and Passion for Untold Success*. Palo Alto: Davies-Black, 2002.

Johnson, Spencer, M.D. *Who Moved My Cheese?* New York: G.P. Putnam's Sons, 1998.

Kanter, Rosaeth Moss. *The Change Masters*. New York: Simon and Schuster, 1983.

O'Toole, James. *Vanguard Management*. Garden City, NY: Doubleday, 1985.

Peters, Tom. *Thriving on Chaos*. New York: Alfred A. Knopf, 1987.

Waterman, Robert H., Jr. *The Renewal Factor*. Toronto: Bantam Books, 1987.

ENDNOTES

1 John William Gardner, *On Leadership* (New York: The Free Press, Inc. Pgs. 1990), 3-4.

2 John P. Kotter, *On What Leaders Really Do* (Boston: Harvard Business Review Book, 1999), 16.

3 Joe D. Batten, *Tough-Minded Leadership* (New York: American Management Association, 1989), 2.

4 Gardner, *On Leadership*, 1.

5 James C. Collins and Jerry I. Porras, *Built to Last: Successful Habits of Visionary Companies* (New York: Harper Collins, 1994), 213.

6 John P. Kotter, *The Leadership Factor* (New York: The Free Press, 1988), 124.

7 Saul W. Gellerman, *Management By Motivation* (New York: American Management Association, 1968), 23.

8 Morimasa Agawa, *Pana Management* (Tokyo: PHP Institute, 1990), 47.

9 John C. Maxwell, *The Twenty-One Irrefutable Laws of Leadership: Follow them and People Will Follow You*, (Nashville: Thomas Nelson, 1998), 101.

[10] Allan J. Cox, *The Making of The Achiever* (New York: Dodd, Meade, 1985), 12.

[11] Warren G. Bennis, *On Becoming a Leader* (Reading: Addison-Wesley, 1989), 163.

[12] Beverly A. Potter, *Changing Performance on the Job* (New York: American Management Associations Publications Group, 1980), 67.

[13] Thomas Gordon, *Leader Effectiveness Training* (Solana Beach: Wyden Books, 1977), 20.

[14] Augustine R. Norman; *Augustine's Law* (New York: Viking Penguin, 1983, 1986), 363.

[15] Joe D. Batten, *Tough-Minded Leadership* (New York: American Management Association, 1989), 142.

[16] Nicolo Machiavelli, *The Prince* (New York: The New American Library of World Literature, 1952), 49.

[17] James C. Collins, *Good to* Great; Why Some Companies Make the Leap...and Others Don't (New York: Harper Collins, 2001), 41.

[18] Henry Mintzberg, *The Structuring of Organizations* (Englewood Cliffs: Prentice Hall, 1979), 83.

[19] Richard A. Fear, *The Evaluation Interview* (New York: McGraw-Hill, 1978, 12.

[20] Collins, *Good to Great*, 126.

[21] Andrew S. Grove, *High Output Management* (New York: Random House, 1983), 203.

[22] Jay W. Lorsch and Thomas J. Tierney, *Aligning the Stars* (Boston: Harvard Business School Press, 2002), 2.

[23] Stephen R. Covey, *Principle-Centered Leadership* (New York: Simon and Schuster, 1992), 246.

[24] Harry Levinson, *The Exceptional Executive, A Psychological Conception* (London: Oxford University Press, 1968, 1970), 133.

[25] Gordon, *Leader Effectiveness Training*, 8.

[26] Kenneth Blanchard, Patricia Zigarmi, and Drea Zigarmi, *Leadership and the One Minute Manager* (New York: Blanchard Management Corporation, 1985), 53.

[27] Marcus Buckingham and Curt Coffman, *First, Break All the Rules: What the World's Greatest Managers Do Differently* (New York: Simon and Schuster, 1999), 57.

[28] Douglas McGregor, *The Human Side of Enterprise* (New York: McGraw-Hill, 1978), 87.

[29] Andrew S. Grove, *High Output Management* (New York: Random House, 1983), 188.

[30] Augustine, *Augustine's Law,* 364.

[31] David A. Heenan, *Double Lives: Crafting Your Life Work and Passion for Untold Success,* (Palo Alto: Davies–Black, 2002), 222.

[32] John W. Gardner, *The Individual and the Innovative Society;* (New York: W.W Norton, 1995), 10.

[33] John P., Kotter, *Leading Change* (Boston: Harvard Business School Press, 1996), 185.

[34] Spencer Johnson, *Who Moved My Cheese? An Amazing Way to Deal With Change in Your Work and Your Life* (New York: G.P. Putman's Sons, 1998), 60.

[35] Masaaki Imai, *Kaizen,* (New York: McGraw-Hill, 1986), 3.

ABOUT THE AUTHOR

Gerald M. Czarnecki is Chairman and Chief Executive Officer of The Deltennium Group, a diversified holding company with interests in retail services, business-to-business services, franchising, trust administrative services, paralegal services, and consumer financial services. He has had a diverse career as a change agent with responsibilities in a range of different industries from retail merchandising, consumer banking, retail financial services, and operations and technology. He has "been there and done that" at every level in an organization from hands-on experience at the lowest levels of leadership to executive management assignments as general manager, chief financial officer, chief operating officer, and chief executive officer of organizations ranging from small entrepreneurial companies to large New York Stock Exchange corporations.

Mr. Czarnecki speaks frequently on the subjects of leadership, marketing, corporate strategy, financial analysis, franchising, corporate governance, and change management for people in both their personal and professional lives. He focuses much of his attention on helping first and second-line operating managers become leaders of people rather than just managers who administer or manage processes. His most popular seminar, *You're In Charge...What Now?*, provides leaders with seven steps to success, all of which tie to the mnemonic LEADERS contained in this book.

Mr. Czarnecki holds a B.S. in Economics from Temple University and a M.A. in Economics from Michigan State University, a Doctor of Humane Letters from National University, and is a Certified Public Accountant. He has been a frequent speaker at industry meetings, has written many journal articles on general management activities and has been an adjunct professor on a number of related of topics at six universities. He serves as a member of the board of directors of State Farm—where he is also the Chairman of the Audit Committee—is Chairman of the Board of Directors of Renaissance Inc., is a member of the Board of Directors of State Farm Bank, State Farm Fire & Casualty, ATM National, Inc., and is on the Advisory Board of CFM Partners, Inc., Private Capital, Inc., and Future Keys, Inc. In addition he is a board member, secretary, and Chairman of the Investment Committee of National University along with being a board member of Junior Achievement, Inc. and Chairman of its Human Resources Committee.

The Deltennium Group
Seminars for Work Leaders

Our Mission is to increase stakeholder value by enhancing the performance skills of all Work Leaders.

Gerald M. Czarnecki conducts seminars on a broad range of business topics including a major emphasis on leadership at every level. His most popular seminar, which reinforces and supports the key learning in this book, is titled: *You're in Charge...What Now?*

This high-energy session is designed to give participants a strong reinforcement of the principles in this book. The seminar emphasizes the need for all who are "in charge" to focus on leading people rather than simply managing process.

The format is highly interactive and provides practical exercises and role-playing experiences that will help make the seven L-E-A-D-E-R-S steps to success, a part of the daily routine for all Work Leaders.

To contact **The Deltennium Group**

Phone: (301) 657-0752

Toll Free: 866-WorkLeaders or (866) 967-5532

Fax: (301) 657-0754

E-mail: gmczar@workleaders.com

Web site: www.workleaders.com